# HOLINESS, TRUTH AND THE PRESENCE *of* GOD

# HOLINESS, TRUTH AND THE PRESENCE of GOD

## FRANCIS FRANGIPANE

CHARISMA
HOUSE

HOLINESS, TRUTH, AND THE PRESENCE OF GOD by Francis Frangipane
Published by Charisma House
Charisma Media/Charisma House Book Group
600 Rinehart Road, Lake Mary, Florida 32746
www.charismahouse.com

Cover design by Rachel Lopez

Visit the author's website at www.frangipane.org.

Library of Congress Cataloging-in-Publication Data:
Frangipane, Francis.
  Holiness, truth, and the presence of God / Francis Frangipane.
      p. cm.
  ISBN 978-1-61638-203-2 (trade paper) -- ISBN 978-1-61638-405-0
(e-book) 1. Holiness--Christianity. 2. Christian life. I. Title.
  BT767.F79 2011
  248.4--dc22
                                                          2010043723

Previously published as *Holiness, Truth, and the Presence of God*, ISBN 978-0-9629249-1-2, copyright © 1986 by Arrow Publications.

20 21 22 23 24 — 16 15 14 13 12
Printed in the United States of America

# CONTENTS

# INTRODUCTION

FOR THOSE WHO are expecting to find in this book a list of rules, I will tell you beforehand, there isn't one. The holiness we are seeking goes much deeper than merely cleaning the outside of our cup (Luke 11:39). We are not seeking an antidote that deals with the effects but not the cause of our human condition. We are seeking the living God, for true holiness does not come from following rules; it comes from following Christ.

The path toward true holiness, therefore, is a path full of both life and death, perils and blessings. It is a path upon which you will be challenged, empowered, provoked, and crucified. But you will not be disappointed. If it is God you seek, it is God you will find.

You may also discover things in this book that you will question. I do not presume to have written without error. Much effort has been given to present the truth of Christ without flaw, but I will be deeply indebted to those saints who are kind enough to share their insights with me. If suited, I will add those corrections in a subsequent revision.

One last thing: our minds tend to justify everything we believe, whether it is true or not. The final proof that our doctrines are correct is evidenced in our lives: "The one who says he abides in Him ought himself to walk in the same manner as He walked" (1 John 2:6). The thrust of these messages is geared toward those who desire the holy, powerful life of Jesus Christ.

If your goals are less than Christlikeness, the benefits of reading this book will be proportionally diminished. Indeed, no one who is content with himself will pass far into these pages. But for you who apply yourselves to these principles, I entrust you to the grace of God, who alone will empower you toward your goal of true holiness.

—FRANCIS FRANGIPANE

# PART ONE

## THE BEGINNING OF HOLINESS

 CB

Think of yourself as one about to take a journey. Like all expeditions, our journey starts with a departure. Long before we ever arrive at holiness, we must depart from self-righteousness and pride. If we would truly live in the presence of God, we must first travel the way of humility and truth.

*Chapter 1*

# HUMILITY PRECEDES HOLINESS

*The bigger I grow in God, the smaller I become.*

[ ALLEN BOND ]

## A Holy Man Is a Humble Man

L EARN OF ME; for I am meek and lowly in heart" (Matt. 11:29, KJV). The holiest, most powerful voice that ever spoke described Himself as "meek and lowly in heart." Why begin a message on holiness with a quote concerning humility? Simply because *holiness is the product of grace*, and God gives grace only to the humble.

It is vital we understand that Jesus did not condemn sinners; He condemned hypocrites. A hypocrite is a person who excuses his own sin while condemning the sins of another. He is not merely "two-faced," for even the best of us must work at single-mindedness in all instances. *A hypocrite, therefore, is one who refuses to admit he is, at times, two-faced, thereby pretending a righteousness that he fails to live.*

Indeed, the hypocrite does not discern his hypocrisy, for he cannot perceive flaws within himself. Rarely does

1

he actually deal with the corruption in his heart. Since he seeks no mercy, he has no mercy to give; since he is always under God's judgment, judging is what comes through him.

We cannot remain hypocrites and at the same time find holiness. Therefore, the first step we truly take toward sanctification is to admit we are not as holy as we would like to appear. This first step is called humility.

In our desire to know God, we must discern this about the Almighty: He resists the proud, but His grace is drawn to the humble. Humility brings grace to our need, and grace alone can change our hearts. *Humility, therefore, is the substructure of transformation. It is the essence of all virtues.*

At some phase in each of our lives, we all will be confronted with the impurities of our hearts. The Holy Spirit reveals our sinfulness, not to condemn us but to establish humility and deepen the knowledge of our personal need for grace. It is at this crossroad that both holy men and hypocrites are bred. Those who become holy see their need and fall prostrate before God for deliverance. Those who become hypocrites are they who, in seeing their sin, excuse it and thus remain intact. Though all men must eventually stand at this junction, few are they who embrace the voice of truth; few are they indeed who will walk humbly toward true holiness.

Therefore, sanctification starts not with rules but with the forsaking of pride. Purity begins with our determined refusal to hide from the condition of our hearts. Out of self-discovery comes forth humility, and in meekness true holiness grows.

If we are not enlightened to the depravity of our old nature, we become "Christian Pharisees," hypocrites, full of contempt and self-righteousness. Did not our Master warn of those who "trusted in themselves that they were righteous, and viewed others with contempt" (Luke 18:9)? Every time we judge another Christian, we do so with an attitude of self-righteousness. Each time we criticize another church, contempt is the motive behind our words. The irony of our Christianity is that so many churches look upon each other with identical attitudes of superiority. *The modern church has become overstocked with those who, thinking they were holy, have become the exact opposite of holiness because they so lack humility!*

Yet the humility we seek is drawn from a well that goes deeper than the awareness of our needs. Even in times of spiritual fullness, we must delight in weakness, knowing all strength is the product of God's grace. The humility we hope to find must go beyond the pattern of living proud lives, interrupted momentarily by intervals of self-abasement. Meekness must become our way of life. Like Jesus, we must delight in becoming "lowly in heart." Like Jesus, His disciples are humble by choice.

## Anyone Can Judge, but Can You Save?

Hypocrites love to judge; it makes them feel superior. But it shall not be so with you. You must seek earnestly for lowliness of heart. Many zealous but proud Christians failed to reach holiness because they presumed they were called to judge others.

Jesus Christ did not come to condemn the world but to save the world. Anyone can pass judgment, but can they save? Can they lay down their lives in love, intercession, and faith for the one judged? Can they target an area of need and—rather than criticizing—fast and pray, asking God to supply the very virtue they feel is lacking? And then, can they persevere in love-motivated prayer until that fallen area blooms in godliness? Such is the life Christ commands we follow!

To judge after the flesh requires but one eye and a carnal mind. On the other hand, it takes the loving faithfulness of Christ to redeem and save. One act of His love revealed through us will do more to warm cold hearts than the sum of all our pompous criticisms. Therefore, grow in love and excel in mercy, and you will have a clearer perception into the essence of holiness, for it is the nature of God, who is love.

One may argue, "But Jesus condemned sin." Yes, and we condemn sin also, but the sin we must condemn first is the sin of judging others, for it obscures our vision from discerning sin in ourselves (Matt. 7:5). Understand this: *we will never become holy by criticizing others, nor is anyone brought nearer to God through finding fault!*

If we are honestly pursuing our sanctification, we will soon discover we have no time for judging others. Indeed, being in need of mercy, we will seek eagerly for opportunities to be merciful to others.

Yes, Scripture tells us that Jesus judged men in certain situations, but His *motive* was always to save. His love was perfectly committed to the one He judged. When our love toward another is such that we can honestly say, like Christ, "I will never desert you, nor will I ever for-sake you" (Heb. 13:5), our powers of discernment will be likewise perfected, for it is love alone that gives us pure motives in judgment (1 John 4:16–17).

Do you still insist on finding fault? Beware, Christ's standard of judgment is high: "He who is without sin among you, let him be the first to throw a stone" (John 8:7). Indeed, speak out against unrighteousness, but be motivated by the love of Jesus. Remember, it is written, "While we were yet sinners, Christ died for us" (Rom. 5:8). *In the kingdom of God, unless you are first committed to die for people, you are not permitted to judge them.*

It is also important to note that the ears listening to gossip or criticism are as guilty as the mouth speaking it. Do not contribute to such sins. Instead, stop the offender from speaking and entreat him to intercede, as Jesus does, for that person or situation. Your ears are holy; do not let them come into agreement with the accuser of the brethren (Rev. 12:10).

Remember, Christ did not condemn sinners; He condemned hypocrites. He numbered Himself *with* sinners—bearing our sins and sorrows (Isa. 53). This is the humility we are seeking. Indeed, holiness shines brightly through the meek and lowly of heart.

## Chapter 2

# FIND GOD!

*There is only one thing that keeps most churches from prospering spiritually. They have yet to find God.*

## Holiness Comes From
## Seeking the Glory of God

H OW CAN YOU believe, when you receive glory from one another, and you do not seek the glory that is from the one and only God?" (John 5:44). If we are displaying our spirituality to impress men, still seeking honor from others, still living to appear righteous or special or "anointed" before people, can we honestly say we have been walking near to the living God? We know we are relating correctly to God when our hunger for His glory causes us to forsake the praise of men.

Does not all glory fade in the light of His glory? Even as Jesus challenged the genuineness of the Pharisees' faith, so He challenges us: "How can you believe, when you receive glory from one another?"

What a weak comfort is the praise of men. Upon such a frail ledge do we mortals build our happiness. Consider: within but a few days after the Lycaonians attempted to *worship* Paul, they were congratulating themselves for having stoned him (Acts 14:11–19). Consider: was it not the same city whose songs and praise welcomed Jesus as "King...gentle, and mounted on a donkey" (Matt. 21:5–9) that roared, "Crucify Him!" less than one week later (Luke 23:21)? To seek the praise of men is to be tossed upon such a sea of instability!

We must ask ourselves, whose glory do we seek in life, God's or our own? Jesus said, "He who speaks from himself seeks his own glory" (John 7:18). When we speak from ourselves and of ourselves, are we not seeking to solicit from men the praise that belongs only to God? To seek our glory is to fall headlong into vanity and deception. "But," Jesus continued, "He who is seeking the glory of the One who sent Him, He is true, and there is no unrighteousness in Him" (v. 18). The same quality of heart that made Christ's intentions true must become our standard as well. *For only to the degree that we are seeking the glory of God are our motivations true! Only to the degree that we abide in the glory of Him who sends us is there no unrighteousness in our hearts!*

Therefore, let us give ourselves to seeking the glory of God, and let us do so until we find Him. As we behold the nature of Christ, as our eyes see *Him*, like Job we "abhor" ourselves and "repent in dust and ashes" (Job 42:6, KJV). As we are bathed in His glory, we shall be washed from seeking the glory of man.

If we truly find Him, no one will have to tell us to be humble. No one need convince us our old natures are as filthy rags. As we truly find God, the things that are so highly esteemed among men will become detestable in our sight (Luke 16:15).

What could be more important than finding God? Take a day, a week, or a month and do nothing but seek Him, persisting until you find Him. He has promised, "You will seek Me and find Me when you search for Me with all your heart" (Jer. 29:13). Find God, and once you have Him, determine to live the rest of your life in pursuit of His glory. As you touch Him, something will come alive in you: something eternal, *someone Almighty*! Instead of looking down on people, you will seek to lift them up. You will dwell in the presence of God. And you will be holy, for *He* is holy.

# Chapter 3

# THE TENT OF MEETING

*When You said, "Seek My face," my heart said to You, "Your face, O LORD, I shall seek."*

[ PSALM 27:8 ]

## A Time to Seek God

THERE ARE CERTAIN times when the Lord calls us out of the routine of our daily lives. These are special seasons where His only command is, "Seek My face." He has something precious and vitally important to give us that the familiar pattern of our daily devotions cannot accommodate. During such times people are often delivered of sins that have plagued them for years; others discover a depth in their walk with God that leads to greater effectiveness in ministry and prayer; still others experience breakthroughs in their families and are used by God to see loved ones brought into the kingdom.

Yet here we are not seeking God for things or even for other people. We are seeking God for Himself. Maturity starts as we break the cycle of seeking God only during hardship; holiness begins the moment we seek God for Himself. A touch from God is wonderful, but we are in pursuit of more than just an experience—more than "goose bumps and tears." *We are seeking to abide with Christ, where we are continually aware of His fullness within us, where His presence dwells in us in glory.*

How do we enter this sacred place? If we study the life of Moses, we will see how he sought God and lived in fellowship with Him.

> Now Moses used to take the tent and pitch it outside the camp, a good distance from the camp, and he called it the tent of meeting. And everyone who sought the LORD would go out to the tent of meeting which was outside the camp.
>
> —EXODUS 33:7

Notice that "everyone who sought the LORD would go out." If we are going to truly seek the Lord, we must "go out," as did Moses and those who sought the Lord. We must pitch our tent "a good distance from the camp." What camp is this? For Moses, as well as for us, it is the "camp of familiarity."

Is there inherently anything wrong or sinful with the things that are familiar? No, not in themselves, but you will remember that when Jesus told His disciples to follow Him, He called them to leave the familiar pattern of their lives for extended periods and be alone with Him (Matt. 19:27; Luke 14:33). Why? Because He knew that men, by nature, are unconsciously governed by the familiar. If He would expand us to receive the eternal, He must rescue us from the limitations of the temporal.

This is not to say we neglect our families or that we become irresponsible as we seek God. No. God has given everyone enough time to seek Him. It is there. Having done what love would have us do for our families, we simply say no to every other voice but God's. We must redeem the time: cancel hobbies, forsake television, and put away the newspaper and magazines. Those who would find God find time.

Sadly, many Christians have no higher goal, no greater aspiration, than to become "normal." Their desires are limited to measuring up to others. Without a true vision of God, we most certainly will perish spiritually! Paul rebuked the church at Corinth because they walked "like mere men" (1 Cor. 3:3). God has more for us than merely becoming better people; He wants to flood our lives with the same power that raised Christ from the dead. We must understand: God does not merely want us "normal"; He wants us Christlike.

For the Holy Spirit to facilitate God's purposes in our lives, He must redefine both our definition of reality and our priorities in life. Christlikeness must become our singular goal.

For most people, however, our sense of reality—and hence our security—is often rooted in the familiar. How difficult it is to grow spiritually if our security is based upon the stability of outward things. Our security must come from God, not circumstances or even relationships. Our sense of reality needs to be rooted in Christ. When it is, the other areas of our lives experience eternal security.

Yet our fears run deep and are numerous. Indeed, most of us pass through life umbilically tied to the protection of the familiar. Experience tells us that many good people remain in lifeless churches simply because they desire the security of familiar faces more than the truth of Christ. Even people who have been delivered from adverse situations are often drawn back into hardship. Why? Because adversity is more familiar to them.

Consider that certain prisoners are repeat offenders simply because they are more accustomed to prison life than freedom. Is it not sadly true that often young girls who have been abused by their fathers unconsciously tend to seek out and marry men who eventually abuse them as their fathers did? Groping blindly through life, they sought for the familiar. It is significant that worldwide most people live within fifty miles of their birthplaces.

Humans are cocooned, insulated against change by the familiar. When we work all day only to come home, watch television, then collapse in bed, our lifestyle becomes a chain of bondage. These things may not necessarily trap us in sin as much as they keep us from God. Moses would leave what was familiar and pitch his tent "outside the camp," where he would then seek the Lord.

> Therefore Jesus also, that He might sanctify the people through His own blood, suffered outside the gate. So, let us go out to Him outside the camp, bearing His reproach. For here we do not have a lasting city, but we are seeking the city which is to come.
>
> —HEBREWS 13:12–14

In the same way that Moses and those who sought the Lord went outside the camp, and as Jesus went outside the camp, so also must we, at times, leave the camp of what seems normal and predictable and begin to seek after God. Here we do not have a lasting city, but we are seeking the city that is to come.

This is one reason why Jesus said, "When you pray, go into your inner room, close your door and pray" (Matt. 6:6). Christ desires us to leave the familiar, distracting world of our senses and abide in the world of our hearts, bearing in mind that the highest goal of prayer is to find God.

Every minute you seek God is a minute enriched with new life and new power from God. Give yourself a minimum amount of time—an hour or two each day—but do not set a limit, as the Lord may draw you to seek Him on into the night. And continue day by day, and week by week, until you have drawn near enough to God that you can hear His voice, becoming confident that He is close enough to you to hear your whisper.

If we are going to become holy, we must sever the chains and restraints—the bondage of desiring just an average life. We will choose to leave the camp of familiarity and place our tent in the presence of God.

*Chapter 4*

# TWO THINGS, TWO THINGS ONLY

*There are so many things to occupy our minds: so many books, so many examples, so many good teachings that deserve our attention, that say, "Here is a truth." But as I have been serving the Lord these past years, He has led me to seek for two things and two things only: to know the heart of God in Christ and to know my own heart in Christ's light.*

## Knowing the Heart of God

I HAVE BEEN SEEKING God, searching to know Him and the depth of His love toward His people. I want to know Christ's heart and the compassions that motivate Him. The Scriptures are plain: Jesus loved people. Mark's Gospel tells us that after Jesus taught and healed the multitudes, they became hungry. In His compassion, Christ saw them as "sheep without a shepherd" (Mark 6:34). It was not enough for Him to heal and teach them; He personally cared for each of them. Their physical well-being, even concerning food, was important to Him.

A lad with five loaves and two fish provided enough for Jesus to work another miracle, but this miracle had to come through Christ's willing but bone-weary body. Consider: Christ brought His disciples out to *rest*, "for there were many people coming and going, and they did not even have time to eat" (v. 31).

Consider: Jesus personally had come to pray and be strengthened, for John the Baptist, Jesus's forerunner, had been beheaded earlier that very week at the hands of Herod. It was in the state of being emotionally and physically depleted that Jesus fed the multitudes—not just once or twice but over and over again: "He kept giving [the bread and the fish] to the disciples to set before them" (v. 41).

*Thousands* of men, women, and children all "ate and were satisfied" (v. 42). Oh, the heart of Jesus! The miracle was for them, but we read of no miracle sustaining Him except the marvelous wonder of a holy love that continually lifted His tired hands with more bread and more fish. Out of increasing weakness He repeatedly gave that others might be renewed.

So, if my quest is to know Him, I must recognize this about Him: Jesus loves people—all people, especially those society ignores. Therefore I must know exactly how far He would travel for men, for that is the same distance He would journey again through me. Indeed, I must know His thoughts concerning illness, poverty, and human suffering. As His servant, I am useless to Him unless I know these things. If I would actually do His will, I must truly know His heart. Therefore, in all my study and times of prayer I am seeking more than just knowledge; I am searching for the heart of God.

## Knowing Our Hearts

At the same time, as I draw closer to the heart of God, the very fire of His presence begins a deep purging work within me. In the vastness of His riches, my poverty appears. The psalmist wrote, "Who may ascend into the hill of the LORD? And who may stand in His holy place? He who has clean hands and a pure heart, who has not lifted up his soul to falsehood and has not sworn deceitfully" (Ps. 24:3–4).

We cannot even find the hill of the Lord, much less ascend it, if there is deceit in our heart. How does one serve in God's holy place if his soul is unclean? *It is only the pure in heart who perceive God.* To ascend toward God is to walk into a furnace of truth where falsehood is extracted from our souls. To abide in the holy place we must dwell in honesty, even when a lie might seem to save us. Each ascending step upon the hill of God is a thrusting of our souls into greater transparency, a more perfect view into the motives of our hearts.

It is this upward call of God that we pursue. Yet the soul within us is hidden, crouching in fear and darkness, living in a world of untruths and illusions. This is our inner man, the soul God seeks to save. Have you discovered your true self, the inner person whom truth alone can free? Yes, we seek holiness, but true holiness arises from here; it comes as the Spirit of Truth unveils the hidden places in our hearts. Indeed, it is *truthfulness* that leads to *holiness*.

God, grant us a zeal for truth that we may stand in Your holy place!

Men everywhere presume to know the "truth," but they have neither holiness nor power in their lives. Truth must become more than historical doctrine; it must be more than a museum of religious artifacts—mementos from when God once moved. Truth is knowing God's heart as it was revealed in Christ, and it is knowing our own hearts in the light of God's grace.

As members of the human race, we are shrouded in ignorance. Barely do we know our world around us; even less do we know the nature of our own souls. Without realizing it, as we search for God's heart, we are also searching for our own. In truth, it is only in finding Him that we discover ourselves, for we are "in Him."

Yet throughout that searching process, as I position my heart before the Lord, it is with a sense of trembling that I pray the prayer of King David: "Search me, O God, and know my heart; try me and know my anxious thoughts; and see if there be any hurtful way in me, and lead me in the everlasting way" (Ps. 139:23–24).

Let us wash the cosmetics from our souls and look at the unadorned condition of our hearts. I know God has created us eternally complete and perfect in Christ. I believe that. But in John's Revelation, Jesus did not tell the churches they were "perfect in His eyes." No! He revealed to them their true conditions; He told them their sins. Without compromise, He placed on them the demand to be overcomers, each in their own unique and difficult circumstance.

Like them, we must know our need. And like them, the souls we want saved dwell here, in a world system structured by lies, illusions, and rampant corruption. Our old natures are like well-worn shoes in which we relax; we can be in the flesh instantly without even realizing it. The enemies that defeat us are hidden and latent within us! *Thus the Holy Spirit must expose our foes before we can conquer them.*

Concerning man's nature, the prophet Jeremiah wrote, "The heart is more deceitful than all else and is desperately sick; who can understand it?" (Jer. 17:9). Quoting another of David's prayers, a similar cry is heard: "Who can discern his errors? Acquit me of hidden faults. Also keep back Your servant from presumptuous sins; let them not rule over me; then I will be blameless, and I shall be acquitted of great transgression" (Ps. 19:12–13).

There may be errors inside of us that are actually ruling us without our awareness. Do we realize, for instance, how many of our actions are manipulated purely by vanity and the desire to be seen or accepted by others? Are we aware of the fears and apprehensions that unconsciously influence so many of our decisions? We may have serious flaws inside yet still be either too proud or too insecure to admit we need help.

*Concerning ourselves, we think so highly of what we know so little!*

Even outwardly, though we know our camera pose, do we know how we appear when we are laughing or crying, eating or sleeping, talking or angry? The fact is, most of us are ignorant of how we appear outwardly to others; much less do we know ourselves inwardly before God! Our fallen thinking processes automatically justify our actions and rationalize our thoughts. Without the Holy Spirit, we are nearly defenseless against our own innate tendencies toward self-deception.

Therefore, if we would be holy, we must first renounce falsehood. In the light of God's grace, having been justified by faith and washed in the sacrificial blood of Jesus, we need not pretend to be righteous. *We need only to become truthful.*

No condemnation awaits our honesty of heart—no punishment. We have only to repent and confess our sins to have them forgiven and cleansed; if we will love the truth, we shall be delivered from sin and self-deception. Indeed, we need to know two things and two things only: the heart of God in Christ and our own hearts in Christ's light.

# PART TWO

## THE SPIRIT OF GRACE

୧୫

We are seeking a level of holiness
that brings the glory of God into our
lives. For us to reach our goal, we
must not only grasp this truth, but
we must also grasp the means to fulfill it. The means to holiness is grace.
In the words of Jonathan Edwards, the
eighteenth-century revivalist, "Grace
is but glory begun, and glory is but
grace perfected."

## Chapter 5

# WHEN CHRIST IS REVEALED

*If you hear a teaching and feel as though it were unattainable in your condition, you have only heard half the message. You missed the grace that is always resident in the heart of God's truth. Truth without grace is only half true. Remember this always: grace and truth are realized in Jesus Christ (John 1:17). What God's truth demands, His grace will provide.*

## The Process of Knowledge Becoming Experience

WHEN SIMON PETER saw it, he fell down at Jesus' knees, saying, Depart from me; for I am a sinful man, O Lord" (Luke 5:8, KJV). As much as we tell others we desire close fellowship with Jesus, most of us might secretly add, "But not too close, nor too often." When the living Christ draws near to our lives, it is common for men to be overwhelmed by their sinfulness. In the light of His purity, there is something in each of us that cries out like Peter, "Depart from me, for I am a sinful man, O Lord!"

At the same time, in spite of being overwhelmed by our sinfulness, the perversity of our sin nature then quickly exalts itself with our new knowledge (1 Cor. 8:1; 2 Cor. 12:7)! Barely do we glimpse the truth before we are boasting to others of what we now know, as though knowing a truth were the same as living it. When we talk about holiness, both reactions are common.

But the Holy Spirit reveals Christ neither to overwhelm us nor to inflate our egos. The ultimate purpose behind most revelation is that what we behold, we are to become. For as we behold the glory of the Lord, it is mirrored onto our hearts, and, in Paul's words, we are "transformed into the same image" (2 Cor. 3:18).

# Christ Himself Is Our Promised Land

As you mature in the Lord, a time will come when Christ will begin to reveal Himself to you as He is (John 14:21). Such encounters with the Living One are often alarming and full of dread. Do not be misled by the so-called religious experiences published by man, where flowers and baby angels gently unveil a docile shepherd from Heaven. *We are seeking the God of the Scriptures!* Every man who truly met the Lord Jesus Christ was filled with fear and great trembling. Nowhere in the Bible do we see anyone who was not "as a dead man" before the glorified Lord (Job 42; Isa. 6; Ezek. 1; Rev. 1). When we speak of a visitation with Christ, it is an awe-full thing of which we speak.

Yet it is for this very encounter with Jesus that the Spirit prepares us. In spite of our weaknesses and sins, God has set before us an opportunity to dwell with Him in His fullness. It is to this end that the grace of God is working in our lives.

Let us see that what the Promised Land was to the Israelites, Jesus Christ and the kingdom of God is to us. The Jews were called not only to know about the Promised Land but also to dwell in it and make it their home. *So also are we called to dwell in Christ, where God in His kingdom becomes our abiding place.*

The Hebrews had a sustaining hope during their wilderness sojourning, yet the promise of God, by itself, did not enable them to possess their inheritance. A generation watched their parents die because they complained and murmured against the Lord. Only those who learned obedience to the ways and commands of God actually *entered* and possessed their inheritance. Likewise, until we truly possess Jesus Christ—dwelling where He dwells and being trained in the ways of His kingdom— our Christianity is often an experience with hardship and frustration. And in this time of preparation, though many are called, only a few are chosen.

Why are there so few who enter? Because the exodus from the mind to the heart demands we become honest with ourselves. We must face and conquer the giants of sin, condemnation, and ignorance. And as it is with any journey to a distant land, the price to actually travel to that country, to taste its water and breathe its air, far exceeds the price of merely reading of its beauty in a book. Additionally, we must realize that the voice of the majority, being afraid of both the battle and the cost, will be a voice of *discouragement* to anyone who is serious about fulfilling the promises of God. Therefore we must heed carefully the warning of Jesus: "The way is narrow that leads to life, and there are few who find it" (Matt. 7:14).

# The Unfolding of the Kingdom

As the kingdom of God opens before our souls, it always seems more than we can bear and beyond our means to attain it. Such is truth to our perception.

But truth does not stand alone in the kingdom of God. The height of God's truth is balanced by the depth of His grace. As it is written, "Grace and truth were realized through Jesus Christ" (John 1:17). Although the Holy Spirit's purpose is to "guide [us] into all the truth" (John 16:13), it is grace that supports our every step.

God reveals Himself progressively. When we are first saved, we "see" the kingdom from a distance. We know we are going to Heaven when we die. Yet Jesus told Nicodemus that not only would he "see the kingdom of God," but also those born of water and the Spirit would "enter into the kingdom" (John 3:3–5). Our salvation begins with *seeing* the kingdom and expands to *entering* it.

To possess the kingdom, therefore, requires attitudes that are uncommon to most Christians. We must not allow ourselves the false comfort that comes with a new layer of religious information. Let us grasp that the revelation of Christ, once seen, is the swinging open of a door God calls us to enter.

But let us open our eyes to the standard of truth that rises before us. The ancient Greeks had no word for "reality." To them, "truth" and "reality," in essence, were the same. Indeed, the Holy Spirit's purpose is to lead us into "all the truth"—that is, the fullness of the reality of God. (See Ephesians 3:19, AMP.)

But the reality of God is staggering! Peter did not succumb under the convicting power of "religious knowledge"—*he met the reality of Jesus Christ!* On the road to Damascus, Paul was not blinded and devastated by a "new doctrine"—*he met the reality of Jesus Christ!* When John beheld our glorified Lord on Patmos, it was not a "new spiritual insight" that left him slain as a dead man—*he beheld Jesus Christ!*

We are seeking the living God who promised, "You will seek Me and find Me when you search for Me with all your heart" (Jer. 29:13). It is in this explosive revelation of the Eternal that what is temporal within us finally, truly begins to believe. It is for this confrontation with Christ Himself that we need to understand the grace of God.

## The Means to the End: Grace

The revelation of Christ is God's means of transferring to us the actual spiritual substance, the very nature of Christ. Every time the Lord is revealed, two things occur: we see truth (the reality and purity of God) more fully than we dreamed possible, and we see our need of grace more assuredly than before.

In this light, let us reexamine Peter's declaration concerning the Second Coming of Christ and the immediate application it has upon our lives. He wrote, "There-fore...fix your hope completely on the *grace* to be brought to you at the revelation of Jesus Christ" (1 Pet. 1:13, emphasis added).

Our minds must be fixed upon grace; otherwise we will always be overwhelmed and withdrawn from the presence of God. It is only natural that trembling should sweep our souls at His nearness, but it is here we must remind ourselves of God's great mercy and His faithfulness toward us, lest we shrink from Him when He commands that we draw near.

In all things, let us fix our hope upon the grace of God. As we stand in the blaze of His glory, let us remember that the nature of God is love. Let us rejoice that we *belong* to Jesus. He personally receives us to Himself, not as perfect beings but as those whom He seeks to free. From His view, *we are His promised land!* Our iniquities, which have humbled us, shall not "humble" Him. Our sins are the giants He has come to defeat, enabling us to become His place of rest, His inheritance in man.

God Himself has given us as a gift of love to His Son. It is the work of God to cleanse us; our work is to yield to His cleansing and to keep faith in His ability. Be reassured: you have been captured by His love. Because of His love, you can become honest about your weaknesses, face your fears, and bring your sins to the throne of God's great grace. Instead of rebuke, you shall find the hand of God's forgiveness extended toward you.

If we are ever going to attain God's ultimate purpose for our lives, which is the revelation of Christ in us in glory, we are going to have to make it through each successive stage of revelation, each uncovering of His life to us and our lives to Him. We are going to see the truth of Christ and the lie of our old selves, and, instead of being overwhelmed, we will stand in faith knowing the grace of God is upon us. Instead of shuddering and withdrawing when Christ appears, we will know from experience to fix our minds on the grace that accompanies His revelation. We will have learned the secret that what God's truth demands, His grace will supply.

*Chapter 6*

# "I WILL REMEMBER
# THEIR SINS NO MORE"

*Holiness is attained only through an unfolding experience with the grace of God.*

## Removing the Barriers Caused by Sin

HAVE YOU EVER had a close friend but talked critically about him to someone else? The next time you were together, did you notice something almost artificial about your relationship? You were not as open or as honest with him. Because of your sin, there was a small but measurable distance between both of you. Though you may have been ashamed of what you did, if you stayed unrepentant, you actually started to avoid the one you hurt—if not socially, at least with your eyes and heart.

You may have shared a world together beforehand, but now the interpenetration of personalities, the sense of being "at home" in one another's soul, is gone. Unless there is repentance, the distance between you will probably widen until the relationship itself is over. Although neither of you may understand why you drifted apart, the love you possessed died because you sinned and failed to repent.

In the same manner that human relationships are sustained by openness and honesty, so it is also with our relationship with God. When we sin against Him, we unconsciously erect a barrier between Heaven and ourselves. We may still go to church, but a sense of distance and artificiality emerges in our hearts.

Each of those defenses we have erected to keep God out ultimately walls us in, spiritually imprisoning us in our sins. These barriers degenerate into strongholds of demonic oppression. Eventually our walls toward God imprison us outside the Divine Presence, trapping the soul in outer darkness. It is possible that our walls toward God are the very substance of which hell is made.

Yet the love of God is such that He loves us enough to release us not only from our sins but also from the *negative effects* our sin has had upon our fellowship with Him. Mercifully, He promises, "Their sins and their lawless deeds I will remember no more" (Heb. 10:17). Every time we ask for forgiveness, our relationship with Him becomes free and new again.

In one sweeping act of forgiveness—so complete that He promises to not even *remember* what we did wrong—God has provided the eternal payment for each sin we contritely ask Him to forgive. He loves us so much that, while He continues to perfect our attitudes of heart, He also provides a means to keep our relationship with Him genuine and without barriers.

# Jesus Paid the Price

"In Him we have redemption through His blood, the forgiveness of our trespasses, according to the riches of His grace which He lavished on us" (Eph. 1:7–8). What is redemption? Redemption is the "payment of a debt or obligation." There were notes, warrants held against us. We are all debtors to God, but by His death on the cross Jesus satisfied the warrants held against us.

> When you were dead in your transgressions…He made you alive together with Him, having *forgiven* us all our transgressions, having *canceled out* the certificate of debt consisting of decrees against us, which was hostile to us; and *He has taken it out of the way*, having nailed it to the cross.
> —COLOSSIANS 2:13–14, emphasis added

The moment you accepted Jesus into your heart, all the things you ever did wrong—every evil thought, every angry word, and every wicked deed, each of which deserved its own punishment—were stamped REDEEMED: PAID IN FULL by our Father in Heaven. Jesus paid for them all with His blood. He is our *Redeemer*. He paid the price not just for the sins we previously committed but for every sin that we sincerely ask forgiveness for now. All our sins are forever forgiven and forgotten.

Hebrews 10:14 tell us, "For by one offering He has perfected for all time those who are sanctified." And again in Colossians we read:

For it was the Father's good pleasure for all the fullness to dwell in Him, and through Him to reconcile all things to Himself, having made peace through the blood of His cross....And although you were formerly alienated and hostile in mind, engaged in evil deeds, yet He has now reconciled you in His fleshly body through death, in order to present you before Him holy and blameless and beyond reproach.

—COLOSSIANS 1:19–22

As far as the sin issue is concerned, we must grasp the completed work of Christ. "Having been justified by faith, we have peace with God through our Lord Jesus Christ" (Rom. 5:1). From God's eternal perspective, we are freed from sin. It is here in the realm of time, and specifically in our minds, where sin still has a temporary hold. In His great love, however, God is removing even the barriers our sins have created between Himself and us.

It is important to state here that God has not lowered His standard of holiness. However, He knows we will never become holy if we are afraid to draw near to Him, for He alone is holy! Consequently He has forgiven *and* reconciled us to Himself through Jesus. The blood sacrifice of Christ has satisfied the debts of every soul who, through repentance and faith in Jesus, sincerely seeks fellowship with God.

## "I Don't Remember"

How little we understand of eternal redemption! How many times will God forgive you? If you have truly set

33

your heart to follow Him, He will cancel your sins as often as you ask. Will He forgive you of the worst sin you can think of? Yes! You may have to live with the consequences of your misdeed, but the redemptive power of God is such that, even in your sin, there are many things of value to be reclaimed. As for the sin itself, if you deeply and sincerely repent of it, not only will God forgive you, but He also will blot it out of His memory.

Let me share an experience. A certain man of God had been gifted with revelatory insight into people's lives. During an evening service he ministered to a Presbyterian pastor and his wife. By the gift of the Spirit, he revealed the couple's past, uncovered their present situation, and then disclosed to them what was to come. This work of God greatly impressed the couple, and as the prophecies were fulfilled, one month later the Presbyterian minister brought two other pastors, each with their wives, to another service for personal ministry.

The word of knowledge was exceptionally sure that night, and the second minister and his wife marveled at the accuracy and truth in the prophetic word. The third couple stepped forward for ministry, and again the word of knowledge was present. The prophet spoke to the husband, revealing his past, present, and insight into his future. Then the man of God turned to this third minister's wife. As he began to speak of her past, suddenly he stopped. "There was a very serious sin in your past." The woman, with her worst fear upon her, turned pale and closed her eyes. The congregation hushed and moved to the edge of their seats.

The prophet continued, "And I asked the Lord, 'What

was this sin that she committed?' And the Lord answered, '*I don't remember!*'"

The Lord had been faithful to His promise: "I will not remember your sins" (Isa. 43:25). Although many times this minister's wife had asked for cleansing, still she could not believe the depth of God's forgiveness. Christ had placed her sin in the sea of His forgetfulness. He removed it "as far as the east is from the west" (Ps. 103:12). From everywhere but the prison of her own mind, her sin had been paid for and removed. And now, in His great mercy, He removed it from there as well!

Oh, what burdens we carry; what guilt and limitations surround us because we do not accept God's total and perfect forgiveness. In Isaiah we read, "I, even I, am the one who wipes out your transgressions for My own sake, and I will not remember your sins" (Isa. 43:25).

How great is the God we serve. How wonderful is His love toward us. He is our Redeemer, our Savior! If you are willing to forgive others and will but ask Him to forgive you, He will pardon your debts as often as you contritely turn to Him. He promises He will remember your sins no more. He who calls us into His perfection has also provided perfectly for us to approach Him. Holiness is an unfolding relationship with the grace of God.

## Chapter 7

# DRAWING NEAR TO THE HOLY GOD

*The Lord did not cease being holy when the New Testament began; His nature did not change. When Jesus taught His disciples to pray, He began with "Hallowed be Thy name." If we would truly know Him as He is, we need an Old Testament fear of the Lord combined with the New Testament experience of His grace.*

## Understanding God's Holiness

Now when Solomon had finished praying, fire came down from heaven and consumed the burnt offering and the sacrifices, and the glory of the LORD filled the house. The priests could not enter into the house of the LORD because the glory of the LORD filled the LORD's house. All the sons of Israel, seeing the fire come down and the glory of the LORD upon the house, bowed down on the pavement with their faces to the ground, and they worshiped and gave praise to the LORD.

—2 CHRONICLES 7:1–3

W HAT AN UNPARALLELED event in the history of man! After Solomon dedicated the temple, the glory of the Lord descended and filled His house. What was this glory? It was the light, the bursting forth into man's world, of the radiant holiness of God Eternal. It signified that the Lord's actual person had drawn near. So great was this appearance of glory that the priests could not enter the temple. After the fire fell and the Lord's glory filled the temple, we read, "Then the king and all the people offered sacrifice before the LORD. And King Solomon offered a sacrifice of 22,000 oxen and 120,000 sheep" (2 Chron. 7:4–5).

Consider this: the king offered *22,000* oxen and *120,000* sheep. They were not serving an invisible God by faith—they were in the manifested presence of the Creator Himself! Solomon could have offered one million oxen, yet it would not have satisfied the demands of his eyes as he beheld the glory of God! *It is only our fathomless ignorance of who the Lord truly is that suggests a limit on any sacrifice we bring Him.*

As Solomon's offering reveals, the more we see God as He is, the more compelled we are to give Him our all. Yet herein lies a dilemma that every present-day Christian must face: though most know of God intellectually, few know Him in His glory. Our churches tend to be sanctuaries of formality, not of the Divine Presence.

If we are part of that sector of Christianity that has rejected ritualism, in its place we simply offer varying degrees of informality. But where is God? Where is His creative, unlimited power in our gatherings? When was the last time our pastors could not stand to minister because the glory of God overwhelmed them? Such was the revelation of God in the Old Testament.

The Hebrew people knew God was holy—that was both their virtue and their problem, for He was *too* holy for them, as sinful individuals, to face. They served Him without relating in love to Him. For a vast majority of the Jews, their offerings were not born out of an eagerness to seek God's presence as much as they were an effort to satisfy His unalterable justice (Heb. 2:1–2).

The common man never approached God Himself but brought his required offerings to the local priests. The priests, in turn, had a multitude of regulations and preparations that had to be fulfilled before they themselves could approach God. There were daily, weekly, and annual sacrifices, sin offerings, and sacrifices of praise for harvests, as well as assigned offerings for restored health. Whatever the need, when the priests approached the Almighty, they could not come near without the shedding of blood or the offering of grain. They had washings, the burning of incense, and the recitation of certain prayers, all which had to be fulfilled in precise detail with the most exacting adherence to the requirements of the ceremonial law.

To further illustrate the Old Testament perception of God, we are told in Leviticus that Aaron's priestly sons brought a "strange offering" to the Lord. When they did so, "fire came out from the presence of the LORD and consumed them, and they died before the LORD." In consoling Aaron, Moses said, "It is what the LORD spoke, saying, 'By those who come near Me I will be treated as holy.'" And the Scripture says, "So Aaron, therefore, kept silent" (Lev. 10:2–3). In Aaron's mind, the holiness of God justified the instant death of his unholy sons!

Ultimately, the relationship between God and the Hebrews was not one of fellowship; it was almost strictly a matter of proper ritual and obedience to the Law. Other than the prophets and a handful of kings, few lived in harmony with the higher ways of God.

As Christians, through the blood of Jesus, God has opened the way for us to enter the holy place of His presence (Heb. 10:19–22). For the Hebrews, however, only the high priest entered the holy place and then just once a year on the Day of Atonement. Before he entered, a rope was tied around his leg and small bells sewn into his clothing. Thus, in the event he suddenly died or collapsed while in the Holy of Holies, the quieted bells alerted his fellow priests, enabling them to pull him from the sacred room without violating the Law (Exod. 28:35).

What we perceive in the carefulness of the high priest characterizes the attitude of the Old Testament Jew: no one dared approach the holy, living presence of God without perfectly fulfilling the Law. Eventually the Jews stopped writing and speaking the sacred name of God. Even His name was too holy to be uttered in this world.

# Understanding God's Grace

This very sense of God's holiness is one of the main reasons why the first-century church in Jerusalem was so powerful. As Jews, they knew the holiness of God's law. But as Christians, they possessed the knowledge of His grace; they knew personally the Lamb, the perfect sacrifice, who had come and fulfilled the requirements of the law. God, even He whom the Jews worshiped, had taken human form and given *Himself* for sin!

Many Christians the world over celebrate the forgiveness of sins in Christ, but they end their experience with God there. Jews, who knew historically the fearful justice of God, still lived outside the Divine Presence because they did not understand the forgiveness of sins in Christ. *But it is the union of both truths that produces power in our lives and leads us into the reality of God.*

Abraham was about to sacrifice to God his beloved son Isaac. (Remember, anyone who has seen God as He is willingly offers his all.) As they walked up the mountain, Abraham spoke prophetically. He said, "God will provide for Himself the lamb" (Gen. 22:8). While we must be willing to give to God our all, we must remember that our all is not good enough. God has provided His own Son, the perfect Lamb, as access to Himself.

There are many times when we feel unworthy, when we seek to escape from the person of God. In these times the last one we want to face is God in His holiness. But in the midst of our unworthiness, let us call upon the Lord. We can escape *to* God for forgiveness.

When John the Baptist looked at Jesus, he told his disciples, "Behold, the Lamb of God who takes away the sin of the world!" (John 1:29). The Lamb of God has taken away not just the sins of the world but *your* sins as well. Christ's sacrifice is much more than all the bulls and sheep ever offered throughout all of time; He perfectly satisfies the demand of God's holy justice. And while the high priest drew near with fear and terror, we can draw near with confidence through the blood of Christ—so great and complete is the sacrifice God has provided (Heb. 4:16)!

The justice of God's law is holy, but the sacrifice of the Son of God is holier still, for "mercy triumphs over judgment" (James 2:13). The Lord who filled Solomon's temple with His presence will fill, *and is filling*, His people today. We have the inexhaustible sacrifice Himself seated upon the throne of grace—it is He who is calling us to boldly come before Him. Enter, therefore, into His glory by the blood of the Lamb. Let Jesus wash your heart of its sins. For our goal is to live in the presence of the very same holy God who appeared in His glory to the Hebrews!

# PART THREE

## GOD'S POWER IN A HOLY LIFE

❧

There is power in godliness. Jesus was holy, and He was powerful. Paul was holy, and he was powerful. Peter and John were holy, and they were powerful. Beware of those who have a form of godliness but deny the power thereof. A holy life is a powerful life.

# Chapter 8

# HOLINESS PRECEDES POWER

*Many Christians look for shortcuts to the power of God. To try shortcuts is to become, at best, frustrated; at worst, a false teacher or prophet. Listen very carefully: there is tremendous power for us in God but not without holiness. Holiness precedes power.*

## When John Saw Jesus

Then Jesus arrived from Galilee at the Jordan coming to John, to be baptized by him. But John tried to prevent Him, saying, "I have need to be baptized by You, and do You come to me?" But Jesus answering said to him, "Permit it at this time; for in this way it is fitting for us to fulfill all righteousness." Then he permitted Him. After being baptized, Jesus came up immediately from the water; and behold, the heavens were opened, and he saw the Spirit of God descending as a dove and lighting on Him, and behold, a voice out of the heavens said, "This is My beloved Son, in whom I am well-pleased."

—MATTHEW 3:13–17

Let us understand this prophet, John the Baptist. According to the Scriptures, John was filled with the Holy Spirit "while yet in his mother's womb" (Luke 1:15). We are also told his coming was in the spirit and power of Elijah. Historians tell us that John's penetrating, uncompromising ministry led nearly one million people to repentance. Vast multitudes left their cities and towns and went into the wilderness to hear the prophet and be baptized into repentance in preparation for the kingdom of God.

Only Jesus knew the fallen condition of the human heart more perfectly than John. No class of people escaped the Baptist's judgment: soldiers and kings, sinners and religious leaders alike were all brought into the "valley of decision." John's baptism was more than a simple immersion in water. He required a public confession of sins as well as the bringing forth of righteousness (Matt. 3:6, 8).

Jesus testified that John was "more than a prophet." He said, among those born of women, "there has not arisen anyone greater than John" (Matt. 11:9–11). John was a "seer prophet," which meant he had open vision into the spirit realm. He testified that "I *have seen* the Spirit descending as a dove out of heaven" (John 1:32). He *saw* "the wrath to come" (Matt. 3:7). He *witnessed* "the kingdom of heaven" (v. 2). John had insight into the secrets of men's hearts. His vision penetrated the veneer of the well-respected Pharisees; within their souls he saw a "brood of vipers" (v. 7). Understand this about prophets: they are aware of things that are hidden from other men.

But when Jesus came to be baptized, *before* the

heavens opened and the Holy Spirit descended, John saw something that was overwhelming even to his standard of righteousness. He gazed into Jesus's heart, and he saw *no sins, no lies, no lusts*. John saw a level of holiness that, without knowing he was gazing at the Messiah, caused him to utter with astonishment, "I have need to be baptized by You" (v. 14).*

Jesus, as the "Lamb of God" (John 1:36), was without spot or blemish. This is exactly what the prophet beheld in Jesus: *spotless purity of heart.* Christ's virtue took John's breath away! The powerful emanation of Christ's inner purity made John immediately aware of his own need. When John saw Jesus, he discovered a level of righteousness that was higher, purer than his own. This great prophet looked into the heart of Jesus, and in the brightness of Christ's holiness he cried, "I have need."

And so it is with us. Each time we see Jesus, each successive revelation of Christ's purity makes our need more apparent. As Christ's holiness unfolds before us, we cannot but echo the same cry of John the Baptist: *"I have need to be baptized by You!"*

Yet, in the beginning of our walk, we embraced life in our own strength, trusting in our own skills for success and attainment. Yes, we turned to God, but mainly in times of grief or trial. But as the Lord brings us into maturity, what we once considered strengths are actually discovered to be more subtle and, therefore, more dangerous weaknesses. Our pride and self-confidence keep

---

* Some presume John was saying he needed the baptism of the Holy Spirit, but John was filled with the Spirit from "his mother's womb" (Luke 1:15).

us from God's help; the clamor of our many ideas and desires drown the whisper of the still small voice of God. Indeed, in God's eyes, the best of human successes are still "wretched and miserable and poor and blind and naked" (Rev. 3:17).

In time, we discover that all true strength, all true effectiveness—yes, our very holiness itself—begins with discovering our need. We grow weaker, less confident in our abilities. As the outer shell of self-righteousness crumbles, *Jesus Himself* becomes God's answer to every man who cries for holiness and power in his walk.

We may think we have spiritual gifts, we may presume we are holy, we may rejoice with human successes, but until we see Christ and abandon our reliance upon our self-righteousness, all we will ever have, at best, is religion.

Oh, let us grasp this truth with both hands; let it never slip from us. *Jesus Himself is our source of holiness!* We are so eager to do something for Him—anything, as long as we do not have to change inside. God does not need what we can do; He wants what we are. He wants to make us a holy people. Let us not be anxious in this process. Allow Him to do the deep inner work of preparation. Jesus lived thirty years of sinless purity before He did one work of power! His goal was not to do some great work but to please the Father with a holy life.

Hear me; our goal, likewise, is not to become powerful but to become holy with Christ's presence. *God promises to empower that which He first makes holy.* Do you want your Christianity to work? Then seek Jesus Himself as your source and standard of holiness. Do you want to see the power of God in your life? Then seek to know Christ's purity of heart. If we are becoming the people Jesus calls His own, we should be growing in holiness. A mature Christian will be both holy and powerful, but holiness will precede power.

*Chapter 9*

# KEEPING YOUR WAY PURE

*The Scriptures tell us that the Lord is our keeper. To be kept by Him, however, does not mean we will not face temptations, for even Jesus was tempted. Rather, it is in the midst of trials and temptations that God keeps us. And the way He keeps us is through His Word. Therefore, if we would be holy, we must know intimately the Person whom the Bible calls the Word.*

## Treasuring the Word

How can a young man keep his way pure? By keeping it according to Your word. With all my heart I have sought You; do not let me wander from Your commandments. Your word I have treasured in my heart, that I may not sin against You.

—PSALM 119:9–11

THE QUESTION IS not, "How can a young man become pure?", as though purity of heart is impossible for a young man. Rather, the question is, "How can he *keep* his way pure?" Purity of heart can be reached and maintained if we abide in fellowship with God's Word.

No matter what our age may be, we keep our way pure by "keeping it according to [God's] word...[which] I have treasured in my heart" (Ps. 119:9, 11). There is a place beyond knowing a few Bible verses, a place where the living Word of God becomes our most treasured possession. To treasure the Word is to love it, even as it pierces "as far as the division of soul and spirit" (Heb. 4:12).

To treasure the Word is to remain fully vulnerable, even as it judges "the thoughts and intentions of the heart" (v. 12). It exposes our motives. It is the lamp of the Spirit, which illuminates the darkness of our hearts with light. It sets us free from the strongholds of hidden sin. It wounds, but it also heals, penetrating deeply into the very core of our being. The Word of the Lord, united with the Holy Spirit, is the vehicle of our transformation into the image of Christ. Holiness comes to him whose treasure is the Word.

## The Word Is God

Many read the Scriptures simply to reinforce their current beliefs. Although they read the entire Bible, their mind only sees certain doctrines. Instead of believing what they read, they merely read what they already believe. Rarely do they find new truths in the Word. Baptists see from their perspective, Pentecostals and charismatics each have theirs, while Catholics and other denominations often have a completely different emphasis. The same way the Jews were "baptized into Moses" (1 Cor. 10:2), so Christians are often baptized into their denomination. When they are fully indoctrinated, their minds have been immersed into a pool of teaching that leaves them more conformed to the image of their sect than to the likeness of Christ.

But if we would grow in Christ's likeness, we must be baptized into Christ's Spirit, not the spirit or slant of any particular denomination. When one is baptized in Christ, his spirit is actually clothed with Christ (Gal. 3:27). It is Christ's image in holiness and power that a true disciple seeks. We cannot allow ourselves to be inoculated with a dozen or so special Bible verses that merely get us "saved" but leave us immune from the fullness of God. You are a disciple of Jesus Christ: the reality of God's kingdom is found in the combined meaning of all Jesus taught. Therefore you must treasure every word!

The Word is God. The Scriptures are not God, but *the Spirit that breathes through the words is God.* And this Holy Spirit should be honored as God. Therefore, as you seek the Lord, place your Bible at the foot of your bed and kneel as you read; are you not seeking to meet with the Almighty? Pray that you will not merely read intellectually. Rather, ask the Holy Spirit to speak to your heart through the Word.

To be a true disciple, you must tremble when God speaks (Isa. 66:2). Prepare your heart with reverence and worship. As you kneel in humility before the Lord, the Word will be engrafted into your soul, actually becoming a part of your nature (James 1:21).

Again, do not read only to reinforce your established doctrines, although prayerful consideration of another's understanding may be of value. Be prepared to take notes, to write down what the Spirit says, being ever mindful that it is the quickening Spirit, not the letter, that brings life (2 Cor. 3:6).

Read with an attitude of willingness, humility, and repentance, and, even if you cannot fully obey the Word, keep it, holding it in your heart. Right here is where most people fall short. For if the command seems impossible or unreasonable to their minds, they disregard it. But Jesus said, "He who has My commandments and keeps them is the one who loves Me" (John 14:21). Many times, *before you are able to obey the Word, you must make yourself keep it.* God must work in you "both to will and to work" (Phil. 2:13). First God makes you willing, and then He makes you able.

In this process, let the Word pierce you; let it crucify you. Suffer with it, but do not let it go. View every Bible command, every "Thou shalt be" as a promise God will fulfill in your life as you steadfastly keep His Word. And as you keep the Word, treasuring His commandments in your heart, the Word itself will effectually work within you, bringing grace and transformation as you believe.

Each of us needs to stockpile in our minds as much of the Bible as we can. During the first ten years of my walk with God, I began my daily study by reading five chapters in the Pentateuch (the first five books of the Bible). I would then read aloud five psalms, seeking to express in my reading the emotion and faith of the psalmist. I would carefully study one chapter of Proverbs and three chapters in the Prophets. Then I would read three chapters in one of the New Testament Epistles and finally one chapter in the Gospels. In all, I studied about eighteen chapters a day. Reading in this way kept me balanced in the various truths of the Bible.

Perhaps you cannot do as much, but just four chapters a day will complete the whole Bible in less than a year. Whatever approach you decide upon, combine Old and New Testaments in your pursuit. I would keep my pattern diligently until the Holy Spirit began to speak or "breathe" through the Scriptures. When the Spirit spoke, I honored Him by following His leading, being careful to write down all that He taught. The next day I would begin my pattern again by kneeling before the Word, picking up my study where I left off.

Carry a pad and pen with you at all times. At night, put your notebook at your bedside, for God will speak to His beloved, even in his sleep. We are called to *abide* in Him, not just visit with Him.

Ultimately, we must be fully given to the words of Jesus. The Gospels must rise to preeminence above all other books in the Bible. Too often Christians preach Paul or another one of the apostles more than Jesus. Yet Paul taught, "Let the word of Christ richly dwell within you" (Col. 3:16). It was the word of Christ that transformed all the apostles. The apostle John taught, "Anyone who goes too far and does not abide in the teaching of Christ, does not have God" (2 John 9).

We are called to abide in the teaching of Christ. Yet, typically, Christians have spent little time in Christ's words, choosing rather to read about Him than dwell within Him. We have "how-to" books for every facet of existence. We have come to believe that reading books is the essence of Christianity. We are ever learning but never coming to the knowledge of the truth (2 Tim. 3:7). Dear ones, *truth is in Jesus* (Eph. 4:21).

Therefore, we must learn to abide in the teaching of Christ, even while we pursue our study of the rest of the Scriptures. Only Jesus died for our sins; our pursuit of *Him* must become the singular goal of our spiritual endeavors.

You must develop such a listening ear that the Spirit could speak to you anywhere about anything. Honor Him, and He will honor you. Keep the Word in your heart, and He will establish you in holiness before God. He will keep your way pure.

## Chapter 10

# THE HOLY SPIRIT OF TRUTH

*Sanctification does not come automatically. We are told to pray for "the sanctification without which no one will see the Lord" (Heb. 12:14). We must pray for holiness. Without seriously pursuing sanctification, no one will see the Lord. We must heed the words of Jesus, "Blessed are the pure in heart, for they shall see God" (Matt. 5:8).*

## The Process of Becoming Holy

SIN WEARS A cloak of deception. Therefore, the first stage of attaining holiness involves the exposure of our hearts to truth and the cleansing of our hearts from lies. This process of becoming holy is accomplished by the Holy Spirit, and the way the Spirit sanctifies us is with the truth. Once the Spirit breaks the power of deception in our lives, He can break the power of sin.

Jesus described those who bear fruit in the kingdom as having "an honest and good heart, and hold it fast [the Word], and bear fruit with perseverance" (Luke 8:15). The first virtue necessary for fruitfulness to come forth is honesty of heart. *For without a love of the truth, no area of our lives can be corrected.*

The Bible warns us that sin is deceitful (Heb. 3:13). If, prior to sinning, one could display his thoughts upon a screen, the entire sequence of rationalizations and compromises—the decline into deception—would be very apparent. But the process of deception is not apparent. *The enemy's lie enters our minds in whispers, not shouts; it walks in darkness, not light.*

Thus, we must vigilantly take "every thought captive to the obedience of Christ" (2 Cor. 10:5). If we would discern the voice of iniquity, we must recognize its lie when it says, "Your sin is not so bad." For sin engulfs the mind in a cloud of alibis and cover-ups as it seeks to keep itself alive. It twists and distorts the truth, and without plans for repentance it calmly reassures us, "God understands; He'll never judge me."

Should an embarrassing sin nearly be exposed through circumstances or another manner, we thank God that our secret problem remained hidden. As likely as not, however, it was not God who kept the sin hidden; it was the devil. The attitude of Heaven toward sin is plain. We are commanded, "Confess your sins to one another" (James 5:16); our attitude must be renounce "the things hidden because of shame" (2 Cor. 4:2). Confession and exposure bring sin to the light. They break the power of deception.

## Are You Sin's Slave?

"You will know the truth, and the truth will make you free." They answered Him, "We are Abraham's

> descendants and have never yet been enslaved to
> anyone; how is it that You say, 'You will become
> free'?" Jesus answered them, "Truly, truly, I say to
> you, everyone who commits sin is the slave of sin."
> —JOHN 8:32–34

Sin is slavery. When the Lord delivered Israel from Egypt, the Hebrews celebrated their freedom with great joy. Yet inwardly they still thought very much like slaves, not free men. Similarly, Christ has set us free from the tyranny of sin. We are legally free, yet to experience that freedom, we must be renewed in the spirit of our minds.

The Scriptures warn of those who "did not receive the love of the truth so as to be saved" (2 Thess. 2:10). *Salvation is not a religious rite; it is the experience of being saved from that which would otherwise destroy us.* Indeed, Jesus came to "save His people from their sins" (Matt. 1:21). The freedom that comes from knowing the truth is freedom from sin and its consequences (John 8:31–34).

For those who do not love the truth, God allows a "deluding influence" (Greek, "activity of error") to come upon them, "that they will believe what is false, in order that they all may be judged who did not believe the truth, but took pleasure in wickedness" (2 Thess. 2:11–12). Each area of your life where truth is not ruling has for its substitute an "activity of error."

If you are a slave of sexual lust, your thought life and subsequent behavior will be filled with secrecy and condemnation, which is an activity of error in your life. You may look wholesome outwardly, but your mind is clouded by a deluding influence in the area of your sin. If you are a slave of fear, your thoughts and deeds are in a constant state of vigilance against calamity. That vigilance is an activity of error. If you are a slave to your appetite, your many trips to the pantry, as well as the lies you tell others about your "metabolism," are a delusion.

God allows this fallen state of mind because of our stubborn refusal to love the truth so as to be saved. Each area of our lives that is controlled by sin is an aspect of our soul under deception.

We previously read that people "took pleasure in wickedness" (2 Thess. 2:12). In almost all sin there is enough pleasure to make that sin attractive. *If sin were without pleasure, only the mentally deranged would commit it, for sin also contains death.* It is the pleasurable side of sin that deceives us. For what is lust but the perversion of pleasure? If we would experience true salvation, we must desire truth above pleasure, for it is our very lust for pleasure and comfort that deceives us. Yet truth is not the enemy of pleasure but of perversion.

Each time you repent of a sin, a lie that once controlled your life is broken. But if you take pleasure in wickedness, refusing God's kindness, which leads you to repentance, God eventually will give you over to the deception your rebellion has demanded. This is why Jesus taught us to pray, "Do not lead us into temptation, but deliver us from evil" (Matt. 6:13). God does not tempt man with sin. Temptation and evil both are inherent in our old natures. *If we continually, stubbornly refuse to repent for a sin, God gives us over to that which we refuse to surrender.*

Proverbs 29:1 warns, "A man who hardens his neck after

much reproof will suddenly be broken beyond remedy." Paul also warns of those whom "God gave...over in the lusts of their hearts to impurity, so that their bodies would be dishonored among them." Why? Because "they exchanged the truth of God for a lie" (Rom. 1:24–25). Every sin is the exchange of the truth of God for a lie.

Consequently, the more truthful one becomes with himself and God, the more he is delivered from "the deceitfulness of sin" (Heb. 3:13), allowing righteousness to come forth.

# Becoming Blameless

"No lie was found in their mouth; they are blameless" (Rev. 14:5). To become blameless is to be free from false-hood; it is to be delivered from sin and the deception that protects sin. Yet this process of deliverance is not attained if we are only casually committed to the Lord Jesus. We must be dedicated to the way of truth. Indeed, each of us has been conditioned by decades of unbelief, fear, and an unbridled thought life, which has reinforced deception.

Christians, who tend to automatically assume they are the "chosen of God," have reassured themselves that they could not possibly be deceived. *The very thought "I cannot be deceived" is itself a deception!* Let us stay humble and not presume that the *calling* of God and the *choosing* of God are alike. "Many are called," Jesus taught, "but few are chosen" (Matt. 22:14). Many tests await the called before they are equipped by God and become His chosen; not the least of these tests is becoming free from deception.

You see, our natural minds were fashioned in a world where the concept of honesty must be enforced by laws. Within our world the bias of our communications media intentionally distorts the facts, advertisers promise the impossible, and people are held spellbound in the fantasy worlds of movies and books. The lie is everywhere and somewhat in everything, and we must accept the possibility that even in those things of which we are sure, there still might be elements of deception.

We do not realize it, but we need *revelation* to know the truth. People who may appear kind, nice, or flattering have proven unkind, cruel, and deceitful. And we must admit that we often attempt to appear better than we are as well.

This effort to seem one way while inwardly being another has created a world in which the truth is not apparent, where things that are plainly seen by one can be invisible to another. Deception and confusion so fill this world that in order for us to discern what is right, Scriptures command us to "seek" for, "love," and "buy truth" (Prov. 2:1–5; 2 Thess. 2:10; Prov. 23:23).

Jesus prayed, "[Father,] sanctify them in the truth; Your word is truth" (John 17:17). He was saying, "Father, purify them of the lies and illusions of this age through Your penetrating Word." In Ephesians, Paul tells us that Christ sanctifies the church by cleansing her "by the washing of water with the word...that she would be holy and blameless" (Eph. 5:26–27). This, then, embracing the truth and allowing the Word of Truth to do its work of sanctification, cleansing, and purification in our lives is the process through which we become holy. Loving the truth is the beginning of our freedom from sin.

# Chapter 11

# REPENTANCE AND THE
# WAY GOD CALLS HOLY

*Do not despise repentance. Every season of signifi-
cant spiritual growth in your walk with God will
be precipitated by a time of deep repentance.*

## Keeping With Repentance

FAITH IS ESSENTIAL to reach purity of heart, for you
must first believe that holiness is possible or you will
never attempt to reach it. But without repentance, faith is
held hostage by the lawlessness of sin. God will not favor
the faith of a sinful man unless that man is in a state
of repentance. James tells us that "the effectual fervent
prayer of a *righteous* man availeth much" (James 5:16,
KJV, emphasis added). Repentance prepares the heart for
righteousness; it unlocks the power of faith toward God.

There is a serious error in our understanding concerning sin. Certain Bible commentators have casually
declared that *sin* in the Greek Scriptures is merely "missing
the mark." While that is the meaning of the Greek word
for sin, we should note that Jesus was not a Greek, nor
did He speak or teach in Greek. The philosophical Greek

vocabulary had no word for "sin." "Missing the mark" was a term coined to define the broadest use of the word, but it was woefully inadequate in defining the consequences of sin. For the "wages of sin" are death (Rom. 6:23), not merely "missing the mark."

The Old Testament Hebrew is much more descriptive in its definitions of sin and closer to what Jesus actually thought and spoke. To the Jew, *sin* was *awen*, which meant "evil, trouble, misfortune, mischief, grievance, wickedness"; *awon* meant "to twist, pervert, to bend down." Another word, *chata*, did have in one of three definitions the phrase "missing the mark," but clearly, "missing the mark" was a minor definition and out of context with what Jesus taught concerning sin.

When we examine the entire picture concerning Christ's attitude toward sin, we can see it was much worse than just a "bad shot." Indeed, in reference to sin Jesus said, "I tell you...unless you repent, you will all likewise perish" (Luke 13:3, 5). In respect to sin and the kingdom of God, He declared, "If your eye causes you to stumble, throw it out; it is better for you to enter the kingdom of God with one eye, than, having two eyes, to be cast into hell" (Mark 9:47).

Jesus said one roving, adulterous eye can keep you from Heaven. Why pay so high a price for so base a pleasure? *You see, sin is not merely missing the mark; it is missing the kingdom. It is living in death when we could be living in life!*

The purpose of this message is to take us beyond simply feeling sorry we sinned. God wants to bring us into an *attitude* of repentance that persistently returns to Him until the fruit of righteousness comes forth in our lives.

The Bible tells us that prior to the beginning of Christ's ministry, "there came a man sent from God, whose name was John" (John 1:6). John the Baptist was sent from God. His baptism of repentance was not the last event of the old covenant to be completed; it was the first event, *the groundbreaker*, of the new covenant. John was sent by God as a forerunner to Christ's ministry. His unique purpose was to immerse Israel into an attitude of repentance (Acts 19:4). He was called to go before Christ. His task was to "prepare" and "make ready the way of the Lord" (Mark 1:2–3).

*Repentance always precedes the coming forth of the living Christ in a person's life.* To "prepare" and "make ready" is the purpose of repentance. Let us be sure we understand: *John's repentance did not merely make men sorry; it made men ready.*

True repentance is to turn over the soil of the heart for a new planting of concepts and directives. It is a vital aspect in the overall sphere of spiritual maturity. To truly change your mind takes time and effort. John's command to the Jews was to "bear fruit in keeping with your repentance" (Matt. 3:8).

Let us also realize that repentance is not over until fruit is brought forth. In effect, John was saying, "Cease not your turning away from pride until you delight in lowliness. Continue repenting of selfishness until love is natural to you. Do not stop mourning your impurities until you are pure." He demanded men keep with repentance until fruit was manifested. And if you will be holy, you will continue in repentance until you are holy.

The apostle John tells us, "If we confess our sins, He is faithful and righteous to forgive us our sins and to cleanse us from all unrighteousness" (1 John 1:9). Do not hide from your sins; confess them. God's grace and the sacrifice of His Son are enough to cover and forgive any and every sin, but we must ask for forgiveness. We must humble ourselves and, from the heart, submit again to God. Be honest about your sin, and He will cleanse you of it.

An exhortation: persist in your repentance, never doubting the generosity of God's mercy. If God commands us to forgive unconditionally those who sin against us (Matt. 18:21–22), know that God does not require of us more than He demands of Himself. If you sin 490 times in one day, after each time cry to Him for forgiveness. He will both forgive you and cleanse you of sin's effect.

During one period in my life I repeatedly stumbled over the same problem. Grieved and doubting in my heart, I cried out, "Lord! How long will You put up with me?" In a flash of grace and truth He answered, *Until I have perfected you.*

The Scriptures tell us, "Reproofs of instruction are the way of life" (Prov. 6:23, KJV). This is not burdensome except to those who refuse correction. The way of reproof *is* the way of life! Jesus said, "Those whom I love, I reprove and discipline; therefore be zealous and repent" (Rev. 3:19). *It is not God's wrath that speaks to us of repentance; it is His loving-kindness.* We have been promised, "He who began a good work in you will perfect it until the day of Christ Jesus" (Phil. 1:6). As long as we desire to be like Him, His rebuke will be a door into His presence.

If, however, you recoil at the word *repentance*, it is because you do not want to change. You need this message. When the thought of repentance is not shrouded in gloomy images of sackcloth and tears, when correction inspires rejoicing and shouts of praise to God's grace, know that your spirit has truly become pure. It is at this point you are walking the way God calls holy.

# PART FOUR

# FLEEING FALSEHOOD

ଔ

Let us ask ourselves: are we merely seeking to be "saved," or are we seeking to be like Jesus? If our salvation does not center upon the goal of becoming Christlike, we will quickly fall into dead works and empty deception. Our salvation is a Person: the Lord Jesus Christ! And it is being conformed to His image that saves us and makes us holy.

# Chapter 12

# BEWARE: IT IS EASY TO FAKE CHRISTIANITY

*Our experience of Christianity must go beyond just being another interpretation of the Bible; it must expand until our faith in Jesus and our love for Him become a lightning rod for His presence.*

## Prove All Things

BUT EXAMINE EVERYTHING carefully; hold fast to that which is good" (1 Thess. 5:21). Would you buy a car without driving it? Would you purchase a house sight unseen? Of course not! Yet many of us accept various "plans of salvation" that do not really save us from the distresses of hell. In spite of the fact that Jesus came to give us abundant life, we remain sick, sinful, and selfish. A car may look nice, but if it will not drive across town, we should not trust it to take us across the country.

Likewise, if our Christianity does not work in this life where we can test it, it is foolhardy to hope it will successfully transport us into eternity where, if we fail the test, we suffer eternal separation from God.

I do not wish to imply, however, that unless we get

every doctrine right and every interpretation perfect, we will be refused entrance into Heaven. Christianity is more a matter of the heart than the head; it is a maturing of love more than knowledge. *The test of truth is not an intellectual pursuit but whether you are drawing closer, week by week, to knowing and loving Jesus Christ.*

At the same time, we should not be afraid to test what we believe. Paul says, "Test yourselves...examine yourselves! Or do you not recognize this about yourselves, that Jesus Christ is in you—unless indeed you fail the test?" (2 Cor. 13:5).

The power and person of Jesus Christ is in us; to believe in Him is to progressively become like Him. As it is written, "As He is, so also are we in this world" (1 John 4:17). However, if we have been indoctrinated to believe that the kingdom of God—and Christianity itself—does not really have to work, or if the absence of holiness and power fails to trouble us, something is seriously wrong with our concept of truth.

We should seek answers to three very important questions. First: *Is my faith effective?* Do not gloss over that question. Honestly ask yourself if your prayers are being answered and if your life is becoming godly.

Second: *If my doctrines do not work, then why not?* Perhaps your theology is fine but you are lazy. Perhaps you need to turn off the television set and dedicate that time to seek the Lord instead. Or maybe you are very earnest but you have been taught wrong. Either way, you must seek to find out why things are not working for you.

And third: *If I do see the fruit and power of the Holy Spirit revealed in another's life, how did he (or she) receive such grace from God?* Do not be afraid to sit as a disciple under the anointing of another's ministry. The Word tells us, "He who receives a prophet in the name of a prophet shall receive a prophet's reward" (Matt. 10:41). God gives "rewards" of impartation, knowledge, and other spiritual gifts to His servants. *Learn from those whose faith is working.*

The final test of any set of doctrines is seen in the kind of life they produce. As it is written, "By this we know that we are in Him: the one who says he abides in Him ought himself to walk in the same manner as He walked" (1 John 2:5–6). Continual, persistent walking with Christ will produce a life like Christ's. We will walk "even as He did walk" with holiness and power.

The fact is, however, that if the "god" of some of our Christian religions died, most members of those churches would be either too spiritually dead or too physically busy to notice his absence. All too often, Christians accept teachings "by faith"—not faith in the living God but faith that their church doctrines are correct. We unconsciously hope that whoever is teaching us has not made a mistake.

We must recognize the fallibility of all our teachers. Jesus said, "See to it that no one misleads you" (Matt. 24:4). Remaining free from deception is a responsibility each of us must assume as individuals. Without becoming suspicious or mistrusting, in humility let us reexamine what we have been taught. *The virtue of any teaching is in its ability to either equip you to do God's will or empower you to find God's heart. If either objective is missing, the information is not worth your time.*

# The Power of a Godly Life

This lesson is not addressed to "bad people" or sinners; it is for all of us "good people" who have thought being nice was of the same essence as knowing the truth. It is not. We can thank our parents that we are nice, but if we would know the truth, we must seek God and be willing to obey Him.

Five times in Matthew 24 Jesus warned against deception in the last days (vv. 4, 5, 11, 23–24, 26). If we are not at least somewhat troubled by those warnings, it is only because we are guarding our ignorance with arrogance, presuming that our thoughts must be right simply because *we* think them. There are areas in all of our lives that need to be corrected. And unless we can be corrected, unless we are seeking God for an unfolding revelation of His Son, our so-called "faith" may be, in reality, just a lazy indifference, a deception concerning the things of God. *Subconsciously we may actually want a dead religion so we do not have to change.*

Yes, we should accept many things by faith. But faith is not blindly sticking our hand out to be led by another blind man. It is not an excuse to justify impotent doctrines. True faith is freighted with the power of God.

# The Power in Holiness

"This know also, that in the last days perilous times shall come. For men shall be…having a form of godliness, but denying the power thereof" (2 Tim. 3:1–5, KJV). Holiness is powerful. Have you ever met a truly holy man or woman? *There is a power in their godliness.* If, however, one has never known a Christlike soul, it becomes very easy to fake Christianity. Remember this always: being false is natural to the human heart; it is with much effort that we become true. Unless we are reaching for spiritual maturity, our immaturity shapes our perceptions of God. We point to the Almighty and say, "He stopped requiring godliness," when in reality, we have compromised the standards of His kingdom. *Know for certain that the moment we stop obeying God, we start faking Christianity.*

We must understand that the "knowledge of the Lord" is not a ten-week course to be passed; it is an unfolding experience with Jesus Christ. It starts with rebirth and faith in Jesus, but it continues on into Christ's own holiness, power, and perfection.

And as we mature, we begin to realize that the Spirit of Christ is actually within us. The cross emerges off the printed page; it stands upright before us, confronting us with our own Gethsemanes, our own Golgothas—but also our own resurrections through which we ascend spiritually into the true presence of the Lord. With Paul we say:

> I have been crucified with Christ; and it is no longer I who live, but Christ lives in me; and the life which I now live in the flesh I live by faith in the Son of God, who loved me and gave Himself up for me.
>
> —GALATIANS 2:20

Do not let yourself be misled! Place upon your theology the demand that it work—your eternal salvation depends upon it! If Christ is within us, we should be living holy, powerful lives. No excuses. If we are not holy or if there is not the power of godliness in our lives, let us not blame God. As it is written, "Let God be found true, though every man be found a liar" (Rom. 3:4). Let us persevere in seeking God until we find Him, until we discover "what [we are] still lacking" (Matt. 19:20). Let us press on until we "lay hold of that for which also [we were] laid hold of by Christ Jesus" (Phil. 3:12).

How long should we continue to seek Him? If we spent all our lives and all our energies for three minutes of genuine Christlikeness, we would have spent our lives well. We will say like Simeon of old, "Now Lord, You are releasing Your bond-servant to depart in peace, according to Your word; for my eyes have seen Your salvation" (Luke 2:29–30). We do not want to just give mental assent to Christian doctrine; we want to see, have contact with, and live in the experienced reality of Christ's actual presence. The moment we settle for anything less, our Christianity starts becoming false.

*Chapter 13*

# A Heart Without Idols

*When we first come to Jesus, He accepts us just as we are: problems, sins, and all. As our needs are met, however, we gradually discover that God is seeking something from our lives. What He seeks is our worship. But true worship is the consequence, the result, of seeing God as He is. It springs naturally from a soul purified by love; it rises like incense from a heart without idols.*

## The God Whose Name Is Jealous

CHRIST DOES NOT personally destroy the idols of sin and self within us. Rather, He points to them and tells us to destroy them. This message is about repentance. If you withdraw from the sound of that word, it is because you need a fresh cleansing of your soul. In fact, we are talking about a type of repentance that is uncommon to those who only seek forgiveness but not change. We are speaking of deep repentance—a vigilant, *contrite attitude* that refuses to allow sin or self to become an idol in our hearts.

In Exodus we see Christ's view of idols. He warns:

> Watch yourself that you make no covenant with
> the inhabitants of the land into which you are
> going, or it will become a snare in your midst. But
> rather, you are to tear down their altars and smash
> their sacred pillars and cut down their Asherim—
> for you shall not worship any other god, for the
> LORD, whose name is Jealous, is a jealous God.
>
> —EXODUS 34:12–14

There are many aspects to the nature of Christ. He is the Good Shepherd, our deliverer, and our healer. We perceive God through the filter of our need of Him. And thus He has ordained, for He Himself is our one answer to a thousand needs.

But how does Jesus see us? Looking through His eyes, the church is His bride: bone of His bones and flesh of His flesh (Eph. 5:22–32). He has not saved us so we can live for ourselves again; He has saved us for Himself (Col. 1:16). *True salvation is a betrothal. He purifies us for our marriage.* From His perspective, our independent ways are idolatrous. They kindle the fires of His jealousy.

An idol is not an occasional sin; it is something that rules us and makes us its slave. For some, fear is an idol; for others it is lust; for others it is rebellion or pride. *Whatever challenges Jesus's right to our hearts becomes His enemy, which He will confront.* Because of His jealousy toward us as His bride, in regard to these false gods, the Lord demands we destroy these idols ourselves.

From the above scriptures we see that Jesus does not want us to "carefully" take down that hidden altar of sin so we will not break it; rather He commands that we "tear down" what is offensive. He is not politely asking us to dismantle, bolt by bolt, our pillars of pride; instead He demands that we "smash" them to pieces. When He shows us an inner idol, we must demolish it completely. We cannot secretly harbor the slightest intention of ever using that idol again. It must be destroyed.

You may feel you are not worshiping any idols. You do not stand, morning by morning, before a statue of Baal and praise it as your god. Indeed, we do not worship the idols of the ancient heathen. Like everything in our modern world, man has sophisticated idolatry as well. Paul talks of the Antichrist who will appear in the last days as that one "who opposes and exalts himself above every so-called god or object of worship, so that he takes his seat in the temple of God, displaying himself as being God" (2 Thess. 2:4).

Where is the temple of God on the earth—is it a building? Perhaps, but in no other place in Paul's teaching does he refer to the temple of God as anything other than the church. Yet, even if Paul is referring to a man seated as a god in Jerusalem, somewhere in that man's life he had to first think of himself as "being God."

Let us perceive antichrist as did the apostle John, who saw it not only as one who was coming but also as a spiritual enemy that sought to infiltrate and then replace true Christianity (1 John 2:18; 4:3). The antichrist spirit is a religious spirit; it is manifested in that thinking that refuses to be taught and corrected by Christ or anyone else. *The spirit of antichrist is resident in much of the church today, opposing the move of God, displaying itself as being God.*

79

Simply put, the spirit of antichrist is that spirit that exalts *self* as *deity*. You see, the spirit of antichrist is much more subtle than someone suddenly announcing to the world he is the creator. Again, our world is far too sophisticated for that. For us today, we must look for the *influence* of antichrist in our religious traditions: are those traditions founded upon Scripture or upon man? And then, beyond our traditions, in the immediacy of our own hearts, we must discern the *disposition* of the antichrist spirit in the thought structure of our flesh nature. Is there something in your soul that opposes and exalts itself above God, taking its seat in the human temple of God, displaying itself as being God? The resistance in you against God is an idol. It is the most powerful idol in the human heart.

But the false god of self-rule does not stand alone in man. The ancient god Mercury would be hard pressed to keep pace with today's gods of anxiety and haste. The world has taken its bloodlust out of the ancient Roman arenas and put it into violent movies. They have taken the goddesses of fertility from the Greek hillsides, only to idolize sex in our theaters and on our televisions. What mankind has done is move the pagan temples from the high places of the countryside to the hidden places of the human heart.

If we exalt money, status, or sex above the Word of God, we are living in idolatry. Every time we inwardly submit to the strongholds of fear, bitterness, and pride, we are bowing to the rulers of darkness. Each of these idols must be smashed, splintered, and obliterated from the landscape of our hearts.

# "I Am a Jealous God"

"You shall not worship any other god, for the LORD, whose name is Jealous, is a jealous God" (Exod. 34:14). The Lord did not say He was, at times, jealous; He said *His name*, which reveals His *nature*, is Jealous. Right next to His name I AM is His name Jealous. His love is not some ethereal principle of "higher cosmic consciousness." His love is focused upon us, actually jealous for us as individuals. He "calls his own sheep by name" (John 10:3). Jesus knows your name. He loves you personally. The fact that Christ is jealous for us as individuals, caring and providing for each aspect of our lives, and suffered humiliation and death on the cross to pay for our sins demonstrates how great a love it is with which He loves us. He gave all. He deserves all.

His jealousy for us is perfect. It is not the same as human jealousy: petty, possessive, and insecure. He is not sitting in Heaven wringing His hands, wondering what we really think of Him. His jealousy is based upon His pure love for us and His desire to bless us and fulfill our lives in Him. He understands us, yet knowing our weaknesses, He still "jealously desires the Spirit which He has made to dwell in us" (James 4:5). His promise to us is faithful: "I will never leave thee, nor forsake thee" (Heb. 13:5, KJV). He refuses to stop loving us. You may think of yourself as a sinner, as unlovable—as though no one wants you—but Jesus desires you.

Early in my ministry, upon occasion I gave up on certain individuals, people who seemed to me hopelessly unreceptive to God. As the years passed, I would later discover these same individuals were now walking with God. Jesus is faithful. He loves you with a love that is jealous for you as a person.

God knows, however, that in order for you to *experience* His love, the idols of self and sin must be destroyed. And to prove our intentions and love for Him, *He tells us to smash these idols.* Would you be holy? Then remove the idols of self and sin from within you. For holiness exists in a soul purified by love; it exudes like incense from a heart without idols.

*Chapter 14*

# THE IDOL OF
# FALSE KNOWLEDGE

*We do not have to be great thinkers to under-
stand that sin can become an idol, a false god that
demands our obedience. But side by side with sin
is the idol of false knowledge.*

## See to It No One Misleads You

S O MUCH OF our Christian experience is based upon
the assimilation and digestion of knowledge. When
we first come to Christ, our attention is devoted to having
our needs met. Unfortunately our spiritual powers of discernment are underdeveloped, and we often take in false
knowledge that inhibits or actually prevents our growth.
Instead of maturing in the Lord, often we are merely
indoctrinated into the concepts of our first teachers—
and not all those concepts are biblical.

We feel aloof toward churches that adorn their halls
with religious statues and the images of saints. But a false
image of God can become just as set in our minds as a
statue is set in plaster—and it will be just as lifeless. If
our knowledge about God is not charged with the life

and power of God, mere knowledge becomes an idol in our mind.

You and I both have ideas, images of God that are untrue, which the Holy Spirit would remove if we would let Him. These are cultural and doctrinal traditions that have become ingrained in our minds. The power of Christ's life is filtered and proportionally diminished by the number of these wrong images existing within us. Individuals, churches, and even nationalities superimpose their likenesses upon their concepts of God. Poor and rich nations alike suppose that the almighty Creator exists and thinks as they do. They are not serving God but the *image* they have of God. Yet the Living One is not a Caucasian or an African American. He is not a Greek or Jew, a Catholic or a Protestant. He is God! And, as the psalmist wrote, "Our God is in the heavens; He does whatever He pleases" (Ps. 115:3). We cannot "train" the Lord to think like an American. He is the sovereign Creator, the life source of the universe. Although idols are "safer" for our carnal nature than the living God, an idol cannot resurrect us, nor can it heal us when we are ill or free us from the devil and ourselves. *The only reason we tolerate dead idols is because while they cannot help us, neither can they harm us or convict us of sin.* We fail to realize the consequences of harboring idols, that "those who make them will become like them, everyone who trusts in them" (v. 8).

In Matthew 24 Jesus warned about the tremendous powers of deception that would be unleashed in the last days. He began His discourse with the warning, "See to it that no one misleads you" (v. 4). Five times in the next twenty-two verses He repeated His warning, saying many would be misled, declaring there would be "false Christs," "false teachers," and "false prophets," as well as "great signs and wonders, so as to mislead, if possible, even the elect" (v. 24). But in the middle of His prophetic revelation, our Lord declared, "This gospel of the kingdom shall be preached in the whole world as a testimony" (v. 14). Underline the phrase *this gospel*. The gospel, *just as Jesus taught it*, with its power to heal, deliver, and make men holy, will be proclaimed as a testimony, "and then the end will come" (v. 14).

In that same chapter Jesus said, "Heaven and earth will pass away, but My words will not pass away" (v. 35). Jesus knew, and therefore spoke with confidence, that His elect would never compromise His message. And while there is a proliferation of false teachings, deception, lying signs and wonders, pseudo-anointings, and so forth multiplied upon the earth, the gospel of the kingdom of God—Jesus's gospel—is being proclaimed as a witness of His return.

What is this "gospel of the kingdom"? *It is the whole message of Jesus Christ.* It is more demanding, more fulfilling, more holy, and more powerful than the "gospel" of typical American Christianity. According to Jesus, when anyone finds the kingdom of God, "from joy over it he goes and sells all" (Matt. 13:44). Once found, it must be sought first, even before necessary food and clothing, and it is such a priceless treasure that one should rather suffer the loss of a hand or eye than lose the kingdom (Matt. 6:33; Mark 9:47). *It is the gospel that costs us our all but gives us God's best.* In the midst of worldliness, lukewarmness, and outright deceptions, this gospel of the kingdom is the message Jesus said would be proclaimed in the last days.

And if we are listening to something that does not center us firmly upon the path into God's kingdom, if we are not becoming like Jesus in holiness and power, we are being misled, and that misleading knowledge is an idol.

## God Is Greater Than Our Knowledge of Him

Remember, it is highly improbable that everything we have been taught since we first learned of Christ is from Christ. We must not allow our thoughts about God to become as unchangeable as God, for we are in transition, and there is much to learn, relearn, and forget. The Lord wants us to be rooted in Him, not rooted in our ideas about Him. We must be confident enough of His love to be able to uproot a wrong idea; an idol is an idol.

The kingdom of God is not a religion; it is an ever-expanding, all-consuming relationship with Jesus Christ. It is as different from religion as a brilliant angel is from a shadowy ghost. If you think God is religious, always remember: *there was no religion in Eden.* The only temple God dwells within on the earth is the temple of our human bodies. John, in the Book of Revelation, is very plain. He says of Heaven, "I saw no temple in it" (Rev. 21:22).

The Father does not want us to worship or serve something so small that a human, finite mind could envision it. He is greater than our vision of Him. Knowledge is important, but it is merely symbolic; it is only a reflection of reality, never the substance. Our thoughts are helpful, but they are not comprehensive. Even of the Bible itself Jesus said, "You search the Scriptures because you think that in them you have eternal life; it is these that testify about Me; and you are unwilling to come to Me so that you may have life" (John 5:39–40).

Our life does not come from the Bible; it comes from Jesus. Those who wrote the Bible wrote to bear witness of Him. The Old Testament prophets pointed forward to Him; the New Testament authors direct us back to Him. *If we would actually understand what they wrote, we must find whom they found.*

You see, we are not seeking knowledge; we are seeking God! We are not hungering for facts but for fullness (Matt. 5:6). God is greater than man's knowledge of Him. If we truly have approached the living God, our knowledge will stand meekly in the shadow of awe and wonder.

Knowledge informs us that God is eternal, but *eternal* is just a word to us. What quality of life has He that the billions of years in the long, full circle of time have both their beginning and end in Him? Our doctrines tell us He is the Creator, but what kind of power exudes from Him that entire galaxies are created by His words, and by a decree from His mouth, our earth teems with life? We define Him as omnipresent and omniscient, but can you describe with knowledge how He can be in every place at once, and how He could be fully conscious of each of us—even the numbers of hairs on our heads?

Our words about Him are infinitely inadequate to describe His real person. Indeed, compared to the eternal realities that await us, our knowledge is but milk upon which we nurse. At best, our doctrines merely pacify our anxieties and organize our beliefs. But in the reality of His presence, is there not a peace that surpasses understanding, and is there not a love that is beyond knowledge (Phil. 4:7; Eph. 3:19)? How shall we measure and define what Paul calls "the unfathomable riches of Christ" (Eph. 3:8)?

*There is a difference between seeking answers and seeking the Lord. There is a difference between secondhand book knowledge and a firsthand encounter with the Living One. God must become as real, as full, and as all consuming to us as the world was when we were sinners.*

Therefore, the cry of our hearts must be, "Let God be God! Let Him be to us who He truly is!" Right knowledge is vital, but we want more than just knowledge. We want the presence of the Almighty to fill the vacuum of our doctrines with substance, the very substance of Himself.

There is a story about Saint Augustine that may help explain my point. Augustine is considered by many to be the greatest of the Latin fathers and one of the most eminent doctors of the Western church. His writings laid a foundation of Christian thought for over a thousand years. His great works include *Confessions* and *The City of God*. At the end of his life, he lay on his deathbed surrounded by his most intimate friends. His breathing stopped, his heart failed, and a great sense of peace filled the room as he went to be with his Lord. Suddenly, he reopened his eyes; with his ashen face now flushed with light he spoke, *"I have seen the Lord. All I have written is but straw."*

We may have ideas, we may possess fairly accurate scriptural knowledge, we may have had visions and dreams, but everything we think we know is but straw compared to the actual reality of the presence of God. The Lord is bigger, more wonderful, more powerful than the sum of everyone's knowledge about Him. He is God, and "He does whatever He pleases" (Ps. 115:3).

Why are we centering our thoughts and energies upon repentance from idolatry? Because, in the very place where the idols of self and false knowledge dwell, the living God has chosen to bring forth His presence. The true, eternal God cannot be alloyed with the false gods of this age. We cannot serve two masters. *We cannot have His power and holiness in our lives without having Him in our lives.* And if we are not being progressively transformed into His holy and powerful image, we may be serving an idol: the idol of false knowledge.

# PART FIVE

# THE SWEET TASTE OF HOLY FRUIT

ॐ

There is something winsome, something beautifully attractive, about holiness. When we seek holiness, we are seeking to surround ourselves with the joy of Heaven. To live a holy life is to dwell at the source of all true pleasure. It is to experience life from God's perspective, enjoying life as God Himself would.

*Chapter 15*

# HOLINESS IS A TREE RIPE WITH FRUIT

*Holiness…is an essential attribute of God, and what is the glory, luster, and harmony of all His other perfections.**

[ SAMUEL FALLOWS ]

## True and False Holiness

WHILE THE WORD *holiness* means "to be set apart, separate," a possible interpretation of the Hebrew root word for "holiness" is "to be bright; clean, new or fresh; untarnished." Holiness produces separation from sin, but mere separation from sin cannot produce holiness. It is not the absence of sin that produces our sanctification; holiness comes from the presence of God. You may avoid touching what is unclean, but if you are not united through love to the fatherhood of God, you will never know true holiness; all you will have is religion.

---

* Samuel Fallows, ed., *Popular and Critical Bible Encyclopedia and Scriptural Dictionary* (Chicago: Howard-Severance Company, 1910), 821.

Christ in us is our holiness, for as close as our relationship is with Him, to that degree we reflect His holiness.

Whatever you think holiness is, however, remember this: Jesus was the most holy man who ever lived, yet He was totally free from religiosity. What is "religiosity"? It is an attitude that emphasizes form and ritual as the standard of righteousness above pure attitudes of heart. The Pharisees are an example of religiosity.

But before we hastily pass judgment upon the Pharisees, a brief study of their origins will help us avoid their pitfalls. The sect of the Pharisees originated after the Maccabean wars. Therefore to understand the Pharisees, we need to be acquainted with the Maccabees. The Maccabees were a family of godly priests, loyal to the Mosaic Law, who vigorously and successfully fought against pagan influences and occupation in Israel. The Pharisees were the priestly descendants of the Maccabees. For nearly two hundred years they bore the high Maccabean standard ideals of separation from paganism. In fact, their very name *Pharisee* means "the separate."

Until the time just prior to the birth of Christ, the Pharisees were typically the most noble men in Israel. They were righteous, bold, and, upon occasion, martyred for their faith. They were the heirs apparent to the kingdom of God.

But, like any sect whose religious emphasis is not motivated by compassion and love of God, the Pharisees' concept of separation eventually made them aloof and self-righteous toward their fellow man. Though they interacted superficially with the rest of Jewish society, their customs and dress kept them distanced from their brethren, for they considered themselves too holy to be involved with the common aspects of daily living.

As to certain aspects of the Law, the Pharisees kept the Sabbath, they tithed even of their garden herbs, and they bound phylacteries (small boxes containing Scripture verses) to their foreheads and wrists according to the strictest Mosaic commandment (Deut. 6:8). They believed in the resurrection, angels, and spirits (Acts 23:8), and they refused the company of apparently bad or immoral people. Yet the Pharisees neglected weightier aspects of the Law: justice, mercy, and faithfulness (Matt. 23:23). By the time Christ was born, the Pharisees were proud of their image and the honors afforded them as clergy.

To illustrate how self-satisfied the Pharisees had become, let us consider the period of time surrounding the birth of Christ. Their indifference toward this momentous occasion is indicative of how distant they had grown from God and how preoccupied they had become with their religion.

## Where Were the Pharisees When Christ Was Born?

A brilliant, star-like orb rose out of the east, which day by day drew nearer to Jerusalem. As it stood shining above the city, a large caravan that had followed the star from Chaldea entered the city. Entering the gates of Jerusalem came the premier astrologers of Chaldea: the magi. The Scriptures tell us, "Herod the king...was troubled, and all Jerusalem with him" (Matt. 2:3), especially at the announcement of the wise men: "Where is He who has been born King of the Jews? For we saw His star in the east and have come to worship Him" (v. 2).

The Bible explains specifically that Herod inquired of *all* the chief priests and scribes as to the birthplace of the Messiah—it was these very Pharisees who informed him, "Bethlehem." Christ, the hope of Israel, the One Moses wrote concerning, was born—the heavens themselves confirmed the occasion by the appearance of the "star"—yet the Pharisees would not so much as investigate, although Bethlehem was a mere six miles away!

The magi, who were heathen by nature, had traveled over eight hundred miles through deserts and at great expense and peril to satisfy their desire *to worship* (Matt. 2:2)! The Pharisees, on the other hand, who knew the Scriptures and were the heirs of the Law of Moses, showed no interest and sent no delegation, although they could have walked to the birthplace of Christ in less than three hours.

How immovable the Pharisees were from their self-righteous attitude. How fearlessly they resisted the Spirit of God! Vigorously they held to their tradition; how carefully they maintained their image. Consider: on the night they crucified Christ, they refused to enter the Roman Praetorium "so that they would not be defiled" (John 18:28). They kept the details of the Law while crucifying the Lawgiver!

This was their religiosity: they held tighter to their doctrines than they did to God. They loved the audible praises of men more than the approval of the Almighty. They assumed that knowing the Scriptures was as weighty as living them. In short, *they acted like many Christians act today: more concerned with religion than with truly following Jesus.*

And so, before we judge the Pharisees harshly, let us measure ourselves: How do we compare in terms of justice, mercy, and faithfulness? How compassionate are we in our caring for the needy and giving ourselves to see the sinful changed? Indeed, Jesus warned that unless our righteousness exceeds that of the Pharisees, we cannot enter the kingdom of Heaven (Matt. 5:20).

# The Nature of the Holy Spirit

Jesus does not want us to become so religious that we miss God. Christ's virtue and power came from the *Holy* Spirit, not a *religious* spirit. It was the fruit of the Holy Spirit that the Father crowned with power. *Love healed broken bodies. Peace drove out tormenting spirits. Joy released captives from sin.*

Jesus said, "The tree is known by its fruit" (Matt. 12:33). Was Jesus talking about botany? Of course not. Rather, He was speaking with reference to the essential nature of a thing. If you want to know if your doctrines are good, examine the fruit they produce in your life. The Holy Spirit in the life of a believer should produce a holy life.

But what does a holy life look like? The Scriptures tell us, "The fruit of the Spirit is love, joy, peace, patience, kindness, goodness, faithfulness, gentleness, self-control" (Gal. 5:22–23). Therefore as a tree is known by its fruit, so the nature of the Holy Spirit is also revealed, or known, by its fruit. If you think you are walking in the Holy Spirit, in discernment, in gifts, yet lack the love and joy and peace of the Holy Spirit, you may only be walking in a false religious spirit. If you are able to notice how "holy" you are becoming, you are not becoming holy; you are becoming religious. Holiness does not notice itself. Holiness is a tree laden with spiritual fruit, a tree rooted in the presence of God.

Indeed, where religion continues to splinter into divisions and strife, holiness—that is, the essential nature of God—brings forth fruitfulness, healing, and unity. How we need true holiness! For today we live in a world where church is divided from church and believer from believer. If the Holy Spirit were truly ruling, there would be repentance, healing, restoration, and love. There would be true and lasting miracles.

The separation we see in Christianity today is evil. It is a sin that needs to be repented of before Jesus returns. It is religious. There should only be one church in each community: a multifaceted church that, although it meets in different buildings, is yet united in Spirit and love with one another. And there will indeed be another group, a false church, comprised of various isolated camps of people who all presume they alone are right, people who call themselves "The Separate," never realizing that such is the name of the Pharisees.

Remember this: religion is its own god. Jesus never said we were to be "the denomination of the world," a "sect set on a hill." No. He said we were to be the "light of the world. A city [community] set on a hill" (Matt. 5:14). When you are holy, you will be more concerned with people than you are with religion; you will reflect the compassions of your King.

*Chapter 16*

# THE CONVERTING POWER
# OF TRUE HOLINESS

*One of the most common verses in the New Testament reads, "And great multitudes followed Jesus." The Gospel of Matthew alone mentions over twenty distinct instances when vast numbers of people traveled great distances to be with Christ. People saw in Jesus meekness, unlimited power, and perfect love. If we would win souls, people must see in us this same Jesus.*

## When People Saw Jesus

And Jesus called His disciples to Him, and said, "I feel compassion for the people, because they have remained with Me now three days and have nothing to eat."

—MATTHEW 15:32

THERE WERE TWO occasions when Jesus fed the multitudes. The first event occurred in a desolate region of the Judean wilderness, and it lasted one day. During the second event, the multitudes had been with Jesus for three days without food on a hillside near the Sea of Galilee.

The impact Christ had upon the local Jewish society was unprecedented! Their entire economy stopped. No one picked over or sold vegetables in the marketplaces, goats were not milked, gardens were left untended, and relatives watching little children did not know when the parents would return! For three days nothing at all was normal. These local communities left all when they heard Jesus was near. Without forethought, without packing a donkey, without so much as taking extra food or telling those who remained at home when to expect them, four thousand men, plus additional thousands of women and children, spontaneously followed Christ to a "desolate place." Perhaps ten thousand or more people left their villages, but we read of no one complaining that the service was too long, the weather was too hot, or the message was boring. *Whatever they lacked in comfort and convenience was overshadowed by the glory of being with the Son of God.*

How wonderful it must have been to be with Jesus! The first time Christ fed the multitudes, they were so overwhelmed they conspired together to "take Him by force to make Him king" (John 6:15).

Such was Jesus. But a problem exists among many of us. People who do not really know Him seek to represent Him to others. And instead of testifying of His wonderful works, they testify only of their religion. The unsaved do not see Jesus. They hear about church; they are told sin is wrong, lusts are evil, and drunkenness is a terrible shame, but they do not see the love of Jesus. Yes, these things are wrong, but *people must meet the love of Jesus before they will abandon their love of sin.*

Plainly, Jesus called a number of people to silence concerning Himself. There were some whom He told, "See that you tell no one" (Matt. 8:4, also 9:30; 12:16). Others He outright forbade to speak, even though what they spoke was truth (Mark 3:11–12). Still others He warned would be doing great works, yet He neither sent them nor spoke to them, nor did He ever know them (Matt. 7:22–23). Indeed, there are those of whom He spoke whose zeal for converts takes them over "sea and land," yet their proselytes become "twice as much a son of hell" as they themselves are (Matt. 23:15). It is not our goal to discourage any from witnessing but to bring us to the realization that what we are in *attitude* and *deed* is the testimony that will be "known and read by all men" (2 Cor. 3:2). A "witness" is not just that which is "said"; it is also that which is seen. *If we will draw men to Christ in Heaven, they must be eyewitnesses of Christ in us.* But if we have flagrant sin or self-righteousness, our witness is noneffective.

## Let Your Light So Shine

Light, in the Scriptures, symbolizes the outraying purity of the holy God. When our hearts and subsequent actions are pure, the light of God's presence shines through us into this world. It is with this in mind that Jesus tells us to let our light shine before men in such a way that they see our good works and glorify the Father (Matt. 5:16).

If goods works glorify the Father, then bad works bring Him dishonor. Paul tells us that "the name of God is blasphemed among the Gentiles" because of the sins of those who fail to represent Him (Rom. 2:24).

King David was a great witness of the living God to his generation, but when David sinned, his witness became a reproach. In Psalm 51, David's prayer reveals the right attitudes necessary to truly witness for God. He prayed, "Create in me a clean heart, O God, and renew a steadfast spirit within me.... *Then* I will teach transgressors Your ways, and sinners will be converted to You" (Ps. 51:10–13, emphasis added).

You see, the credibility of our witness is lost when sin rules in our lives. The world has heard too many Christians give testimony to a life they are not living. They cause multitudes of people to think Christianity does not work.

## How to Know When to Witness

> But sanctify Christ as Lord in your hearts, always being ready to make a defense to everyone who asks you...for the hope that is in you, yet with gentleness and reverence.
>
> —1 PETER 3:15

Many Christians are told to witness for Jesus. Again, we would not discourage your witness for Jesus; rather we seek to *encourage* you to live for Him as well! *Let people see Him in you before you testify.* There are Christians who publicly sin in the workplace: they lose their tempers and do bad work; they are often late or heard complaining about management and job conditions. Yet they feel compelled to give their testimony. "They profess to know God, but by their deeds they deny Him" (Titus 1:16). A "voice" in their minds compels them to "witness for Jesus." Sometimes that voice is the Holy Spirit, but more often it is not. Undaunted, they are sure it is from Heaven since they feel "guilty" until they witness and "good" afterward.

There is one sure way to know if the "voice" urging you to witness is from God: if the voice speaking to you is the *audible* voice of someone who has seen your good works and is asking about your way of life, that voice has been inspired by God. When people see Christ in you—in your patience when wronged, your peace in adversity, your forgiveness amidst cruelty—they will ask about your hope.

## The Seed of Reproduction Is in Your Fruit

If your conversion is genuine, you found a love for Jesus that is, in itself, a witness of His life. Unfortunately, we often seek to lead people into our religion instead of to Christ. How often we seek to convert our family and friends into a particular church structure. People must be led to Jesus, not merely to church.

Let us always remember, Jesus wants to reach people, not drive them away. How does God expect us to do that? First, let us make sure our conversion is real, that we have truly given over our lives to Jesus Christ. Then, determine to bear the spiritual fruit of love and humility in your life.

In the Garden of Eden the Lord placed trees with

seed in the fruit. *Remember this always: the power to reproduce life is in the fruit.* And for fruit to be edible, it must be mature and sweet. The fruit we must display comes from the tree of life, which brings "healing of the nations" (Rev. 22:2). It is not in the tree of the knowledge of good and evil—legalistic laws, judging what is wrong in people.

If you would like to see reproduced in your loved ones or friends the experienced reality of God, walk in the fruit of the Spirit. *The power of reproduction is in the seed, and the seed is in the fruit.*

And should you sin or stumble before them, which we all do at times, repent both to God and to those you have sinned against. A sincere repentance to an unsaved person is a sure sign that God is both real and in control of your life!

Parents, do you want your children raised for Christ? Do you want your words to impart eternal life? Walk in the fruit of the Holy Spirit. As the fruit in your life nourishes your children, the seeds within your fruitfulness will reproduce in your family the same qualities. Would you convert your spouse? Your parents? Your friends? Walk in the fruit of the Spirit, in love, joy, peace, patience, and kindness. Those who know you will find your life very attractive, for through your life they will see the holy life of Jesus.

*Chapter 17*

# THE HIGHWAY OF HOLINESS

*Why do we think holiness is so full of gloom? The images of strict, joyless rules surrounding the holy life are inconsistent with both the Word and nature of God. God is love. A holy life is a life alive with love, compelled by love, filled with love.*

## The Power and Joy of Love

MOST OF US are afraid to live in the exposed, vulnerable state of heart that love demands. As Christians, we talk about love much more often than we live it. But real love is daring; it is exciting. It boldly conquers evil, then heals and reunites with God those whom it loves. It is aggressive.

The state of love of which we are afraid is that transitory stage where we are learning to forgive. This is the aspect of love that hurts, and its hurt is amplified by our reluctance to forgive. We, like Jesus, must live in a continual attitude of forgiveness; then we can step into the joy and power of aggressive love.

God's love is not just forgiving; it is for living. As we overcome bitterness and climb out of the pit of unforgiveness—suddenly we are as bold as a lion. Love grows from being a commandment to becoming an adventure!

It is the same with joy. The joy that comes to us through the Holy Spirit is a joy that actually becomes our strength! The imprisoned, impoverished state of this world has deceived us into thinking that a life with God is only a life of pain. Jesus compared His ministry to one who "played the flute" (Matt. 11:17). He said His message of grace and the kingdom of God, when it was properly heard, should cause men to "dance" in celebration!

It is true that Jesus suffered in bearing our sins and that there were times of great sobriety when He spoke. But there were many other times when He exhibited great joy. The Scriptures tell us that Jesus "rejoiced greatly in the Holy Spirit" when His disciples returned from a powerful time of evangelism (Luke 10:21). How do you envision Jesus rejoicing? The word *rejoice* that is used here meant "to leap much for joy." Jesus, the King, was leaping for joy!

Isaiah tells us about the way to holiness. Nowhere in the verses do we see any of the gloom hell forecasts for the godly.

> A highway will be there, a roadway,
> And it will be called the Highway of Holiness.
> The unclean will not travel on it,
> But it will be for him who walks that way,
> And fools will not wander on it.
> No lion will be there,
> Nor will any vicious beast go up on it;

These will not be found there.
But the redeemed will walk there,
And the ransomed of the LORD will return,
And come with joyful shouting to Zion,
With everlasting joy upon their heads.
They will find gladness and joy,
And sorrow and sighing will flee away.

—ISAIAH 35:8–10

Behold the way of holiness! Sorrow and sighing flee away! The highway to holiness is the way to *God*, not religion. It is a way of life in which all the judgments, negative consequences, and problems of the sinful, unclean life—those things that brought death into our world— are eliminated from our lives! No unclean...no lion...no vicious beast will be found there. *Much of the spiritual warfare that fed upon our ignorance, unbelief, and sinfulness is simply nonexistent for the holy.*

What is in store for those who walk toward holiness? It is the wonderful, experienced knowledge that we are "redeemed...and the ransomed." What attitude fills our hearts? Three expressions of joy await God's holy ones: "joyful shouting," "everlasting joy upon their heads," and "gladness and joy."

Satan would have us believe Heaven is as gloomy as hell. As we embrace holiness and walk in it, as we strive to live out lives consecrated in heart and mind unto God and separate from the lusts of the world, the Lord crowns us with everlasting joy. Not gloom—joy! Not "sometimes-lasting" joy but *everlasting joy*; not "Sunday-morning-only" joy but *moment-by-moment, eternal joy*!

107

This is no pious sense of religiosity; it is abounding in life. They "shout for joy over their portion" (Isa. 61:7)! This is the end result of holiness. It is nearness to God; it is joy worth shouting about and full of glory!

# PART SIX

# THE RADIANCE OF HOLINESS

CB

The Book of Psalms tells us that God covers Himself "with light as with a garment" (Ps. 104:2, KJV). The apostle John declares, "God is Light" (1 John 1:5). And James refers to the Father as "the Father of lights" (James 1:17). You and I are the "lights" that God has fathered. We are children of God, and, as such, the light of His presence shines within us. As our hearts are purified by truth, the splendor of God's glory expands around us, and like our Father, we also cover ourselves "with light as with a garment."

*Chapter 18*

# A PLACE FOR HIM TO REST

*In the kingdom, there are no great men of God, just humble men whom God has chosen to use greatly. How do we know when we are humble? When God speaks, we tremble. God is looking for a man who trembles at His words. Such a man will find the Spirit of God resting upon him; he will become a dwelling place for the Almighty.*

## Entering the Sabbath Rest of God

Heaven is My throne, and the earth is My footstool. Where then is a house you could build for Me? And where is a place that I may rest?

—ISAIAH 66:1

GOD ASKS FOR nothing but ourselves. Our beautiful church buildings, our slick professionalism, all are nearly useless to God. He does not want what we have; He wants who we are. He seeks to create in our hearts a sanctuary for Himself, a place where He may rest.

In the Scriptures this *rest* is called "a Sabbath rest" (Heb. 4:9). It does not, however, come from keeping the Sabbath, for the Jews kept the Sabbath but never entered

God's rest. The Book of Hebrews is plain: Joshua did not give the Israelites rest (vv. 7–8). And after so long a period of Sabbath-keeping, Scripture continues, "So there remains a Sabbath rest for the people of God" (v. 9).

The question must be asked then, "What is this Sabbath rest?" Let us explore Genesis in pursuit of our answer. "Then God blessed the seventh day and sanctified it, because in it He rested from all His work" (Gen. 2:3). Before God rested on the Sabbath, there was nothing special or holy about the seventh day. Had the Lord rested on the third day, then it would have been holy. *Rest is not in the Sabbath; it is in God.* Rest is a prevailing quality of His completeness.

Revelation 4:6 describes the throne of God as having before it, as it were, "a sea of glass, like crystal." A sea of glass is a sea without waves or ripples, a symbol of the imperturbable calm of God. Let us grasp this point: *the Sabbath was not a source of rest for God; He was the source of rest for the Sabbath.* As it is written, "The Creator of the ends of the earth does not become weary or tired" (Isa. 40:28). And even as the Sabbath became holy when God rested upon it, so we become holy as we put away sin, as the fullness of God settles and rests upon us.

In our study, we are not associating God's rest merely with the sense of being rebuilt or rejuvenated, which we obviously need and associate with human rest. The rest we seek is not a rejuvenation of our energy; it is the *exchange* of energy: our life for God's, through which the vessel of our humanity is filled with the Divine Presence and the all-sufficiency of Christ Himself.

# Enveloped and Permeated With God

The Hebrew word for *rest* is *nuach*; among other things, it means "to rest, remain, be quiet." It also indicates a "complete envelopment and thus permeation," as in the spirit of Elijah "resting" on Elisha, or when wisdom "rests in the heart of him who has understanding." God is not looking for a place where He can merely cease from His labors with men. He seeks a relationship where He can "completely envelop and thus permeate" every dimension of our lives, where He can tabernacle, remain, and be quiet within us.

When God's rest abides upon us, we live in union with Jesus the same way He lived in union with the Father (John 10:14–15). Christ's thought life was "completely enveloped and thus permeated" with the presence of God. He did only those things He saw and heard His Father do. He declared, "The Father abiding in Me does His works" (John 14:10). *There is rest because it is Christ working through us.* Jesus promises us, "If you ask Me anything in My name, I will do it" (v. 14). How vain we are to think we can do miracles, love our enemies, or do any of the works of God without Christ doing the works through us!

This is why Jesus said, "Come to Me...and I will give you rest" (Matt. 11:28). In a storm-tossed boat on the Sea of Galilee, Christ's terrified disciples came to Him. Their cries were the cries of men about to die. Jesus rebuked the tempest, and immediately the wind and sea became "perfectly calm," even as calm as He was (Matt. 8:26). What program, what degree of ministerial professionalism can compare with the life and power we receive through Him?

You see, our efforts, no matter how much we spend of ourselves, cannot produce the rest or life of God. *We must come to Him.* Many leaders have worked themselves nearly to exhaustion seeking to serve God. If they spent half their time *with Him*, in prayer and waiting before Him, they would find His supernatural accompaniment working mightily in their efforts. They would become passengers in the vehicle of His will, a vehicle in which He Himself is both captain and navigator.

## Cease Striving, Know, Then Obey

To enter God's rest requires we abide in full surrender to His will, in perfect trust of His power. We learn to rest from our works "as God did from His" (Heb. 4:10). To "rest from our labors" does not mean we have stopped working; it means we have stopped the laborious work of the flesh and sin. It means we have entered the eternal works that He brings forth through us.

The turmoil caused by unbelief is brought to rest by faith. The strife rooted in unforgiveness is removed by love. Our fearful thoughts, He arrests through trust; our many questions are answered by His wisdom. Such is the mind that has entered the rest of God.

The church needs to possess the knowledge of God's ways, for herein do we enter His rest (Heb. 3:8–12). We gain such knowledge through obedience to God's Word during conflicts. As we obey God through the testings of life, we learn how to deal with situations as God would.

Consequently, it is of the utmost value to hear what God is speaking to us, and especially so when life seems to be a wilderness of hardship and trials.

> Therefore, just as the Holy Spirit says, "Today if you hear His voice, do not harden your hearts as when they provoked Me, as in the day of trial in the wilderness....Therefore I was angry with this generation, and said, 'They always go astray in their heart, and they did not know My ways'; as I swore in My wrath, 'They shall not enter My rest.'"
> —HEBREWS 3:7–8, 10–11

He says, "They always go astray in their heart...they did not know My ways...they shall not enter My rest." Let us understand: *knowing God's ways leads to His rest.*

We must see that there is no rest in a hardened heart. There is no rest when we rebel against God. Our rest comes from becoming honest about our needs and allowing Christ to change us.

Thus Jesus said, "Learn from Me...and you will find rest for your souls" (Matt. 11:29). Stop fighting with God and learn from Him. Let His Word put to death the torments of the sin nature. Cease struggling, cease wrestling against the Blessed One. Trust Him! For eventually His Word will plunder the defenses of your heart. Be committed to your surrender. In time He shall no longer use adversity to reach your heart, for you shall delight in being vulnerable to Him. Continue your diligent yielding until even His whisper brings sweet trembling to your soul. Far more precious than the men of a hundred nations is one man perfectly given to the Spirit of God. This man is God's tabernacle, the one to whom God looks...and with whom He is well pleased.

He says, "Heaven is My throne and the earth is My footstool. Where then is a house you could build for Me? And where is a place that I may rest? For My hand made all these things, thus all these things came into being" (Isa. 66:1–2). Yet, incredibly, one man with one quality of heart captures the attention and promise of God. "But to this one I will look, to him who is humble and contrite of spirit, and who trembles at My word" (v. 2).

God looks to the man who trembles when He speaks. For in him the holy power of the Most High can, without striving, abide in perfect peace. He has learned the ways of God; he delights in obedience. He has chosen to give God what He asks: nothing less than all he is. In return, this man becomes a place, a holy place, where God Himself can rest.

# Chapter 19

# THE BRIGHT LAMP OF HOLINESS

*When true holiness exists in a Christian's life, it produces a luminosity, a glow around that individual. Infants and little children, because their spirits are yet pure and undefiled and because they are so close to the actual presence of God, emanate this light as well. Their light is visible because their hearts are transparent and truthful. For us, the way to the bright lamp of holiness is this same way of transparency and truth. It is the way to the pure gold of the kingdom of God.*

## When Your Eye Is Single

FROM THE MOMENT Christ enters within us, we are holy, set apart unto God. This kind of holiness is the same sanctification that made the utensils in the temple holy: holy because they were used in service to the Lord. They had no virtue in themselves; their material substance did not change. Christianity, in general, is holy in that sense. But the holiness we are seeking is the *fulfillment* of having been set apart. We are seeking a holiness that mirrors, through us, the presence of God in Heaven. We are seeking both His nature and His quality of life.

Since true holiness produces in us the actual life of the Holy Spirit, we must be sure we know who the Spirit is. The Spirit of God is love, not religion. God is life, not rituals. The Holy Spirit does more in us than simply enable us to "speak in tongues" or witness. *The Spirit leads us into the presence of Jesus.* Herein is our holiness received: in our union and fellowship with Jesus Christ.

Again, the holiness we are seeking is not a legislative or legalistic set of rules; it is Christ's very own quality of life. The Holy Spirit works in us not merely a new desire to love, but He imparts to us Christ's very own love. We develop more than just a general faith in Jesus; we actually begin believing *like* Jesus, with *His* quality of faith. It is *God in us* that makes us holy. Let it stagger us, let it rock us off our comfortable little perches until, with great trembling and great joy, with deep worship and holy fear, we approach the divine reality who has, for His own will and purpose, called us to Himself.

"Do you not know that you are a temple of God, and that the Spirit of God dwells in you?" (1 Cor. 3:16). The Spirit of God dwells in us. In this light let us ask ourselves again the age-old question, "What is man?" We know how we appear to other men, but if God truly is within us, how do we appear to angels or devils? What light marks us in the spirit world, what illumination surrounds us, what glory declares to the invisible realm, "Behold and beware, here walks a son of God"? Think of it: the Spirit of the Creator, who purposed in the beginning to make man in His image, is in you...now.

# ، Holiness Is a Body Full of Light

There are limitations. There are conditions. You cannot serve two masters. You cannot serve light and darkness, sin and righteousness, self and God. Light is within you, but so also is darkness. Our world is a world in darkness. Our ancestors were sons of darkness. Our carnal minds yet remain theaters of darkness. In a world of choices we must choose light. That is why Jesus taught that we must be single-minded if we would become fully mature sons of light. He said, "The light of the body is the eye: therefore when thine eye is single, thy whole body also is full of light; but when thine eye is evil, thy body also is full of darkness" (Luke 11:34, KJV).

If you are focused in your will and heart toward God, your body is full of light, and you are giving full expression to the glory of God within you. But if you are double-minded, if you are dwelling on sinful or evil thoughts, your light is proportionally diminished until your very body is full of darkness. Jesus went on to warn, "Take heed therefore that the light which is in thee be not darkness" (v. 35, KJV).

If you do nothing about your salvation, fail to seek God, or choose to disobey Him, you are in darkness. Do not console yourself with an aimless hope that someday, somehow you will get better. Arm yourself with determination! For if the light in you is in darkness, how terrible is that darkness. Son of light, you must *hate* darkness! Darkness is the substance of hell; it is the world without God.

But our hope is light, not darkness. Your feet are

walking the path of the just, the path that grows brighter and brighter unto the full day. "If therefore your whole body is full of light, with no dark part in it, it shall be wholly illumined, as when the lamp illumines you with its rays" (Luke 11:36). This verse gives a very clear picture of what holiness looks like in its maturity: our bodies are radiant with glory even as a lamp shines at full brightness. What a tremendous hope—that we can be so wholly illumined with the presence of God that there is "no dark part" within us. A garment of light and glory awaits the spiritually mature, the holy ones of God, a garment similar to what Jesus wore on the Mount of Transfiguration. It's a splendor not just put on in eternity but one worn here, "in the midst of a crooked and perverse generation"; here, where we "appear as lights in the world" (Phil. 2:15).

"You were formerly darkness, but now you are Light in the Lord; walk as children of Light" (Eph. 5:8). *Now you are a child of light.* These are not merely figures of speech. The glory of God is within and around you; it is a spiritual reality! But what of the darkness that is yet within you? Paul continued:

> Do not participate in the unfruitful deeds of darkness, but instead even expose them....But all things become visible when they are exposed by the light, for everything that becomes visible is light.
>
> —EPHESIANS 5:11, 13

Do not hide your darkness; expose it. Do not sympathetically make excuses for it; confess it. Hate it. Renounce it. For as long as darkness remains in darkness, it rules you. But when you bring darkness out into the light, it becomes light. When you take your secret sins and boldly come unto the throne of God's grace and confess them, He cleanses you from all unrighteousness (1 John 1:9). If you sin again, repent again—and again, until the habit of sin is broken within you.

Like the prospectors of old, you must stake your claim high in the kingdom of God, being ready to defend your rights to the "pure gold" of Heaven (Rev. 3:18). And as you pitch your tent at the throne of grace, something eternal will begin to glow in you, like hot coals on a furnace floor. And as you persist with the Almighty, the sacred fire of His presence will consume the wood, hay, and stubble of your former ways. Power such as Jesus had will reside in your innermost being. Angels will stand in awe, for your gold will be refined, your garments light, and your life holy.

# Chapter 20

# THE WAY INTO THE HOLY PLACE

*In the chronicles of the restoration of the church, it will be noted that a time came when the saints ceased being satisfied with their song services, when the deepest longings of their hearts ascended beyond the sounds of shouts and hand-clapping— a transitional time when pure worship began to carry them into the actual presence of God.*

## We Are the Temple of God

OUR PURSUIT OF God would profit from a brief study of the Book of Hebrews. This book, originally written "to the Hebrews," is a message to people who were familiar with the tabernacle of God and the significance of the Divine Presence in the inner court of the tabernacle. We will be exploring the similarities between the inner and outer courts of the Hebrew tabernacle and the "inner and outer courts" of the New Testament tabernacle: *the Spirit-filled disciple.* Both have a sacred place that was created for the presence of God. And both have a prescribed way to enter the sacred presence.

Paul tells us, "Examine yourselves! Or do you not recognize this about yourselves, that Jesus Christ is in you?" (2 Cor. 13:5). Again we are challenged, "Do you not know that you are a temple of God, and that the Spirit of God dwells in you?" (1 Cor. 3:16). And again Jesus, speaking for both Himself and God the Father, promised, "If anyone loves Me, he will keep My word; and My Father will love him, and We will come to him and make Our abode with him" (John 14:23).

Such statements are so bold that most Bible teachers refuse to deal with them for fear of being accused of heresy. Yet the incredible reality of God's Word cannot be altered in spite of compromise within the church. The holy meaning of the Word stands towering above men's traditions and unbelief. There is an "upward call of God in Christ Jesus" (Phil. 3:14). We will not ignore or rush past any of God's words. Rather, we encourage you to take time with this study, to dwell in it. For if you receive it properly, a door will swing open before you into the secret place of the Most High.

## The Outer and Inner Rooms

*There is a place in your spirit where Christ actually dwells, an abiding place where His Holy Spirit and your human spirit literally touch.* You are eternally saved not because you accepted the religion called Christianity but because you have accepted the actual Spirit of Jesus Christ into your heart. Through Him you are able to come to God.

This is not merely a doctrine of faith; it is a matter of fact. The dwelling of Christ in our spirits is a holy place.

We accept this truth because it is biblical. But how do we gain access to this holy place? And, once entered, is it possible to dwell there continually? The Book of Hebrews provides us with an answer. In chapter 9 we read, "The Holy Spirit is signifying this, that the way into the holy place has not yet been disclosed while the outer tabernacle is still standing" (v. 8).

There is a way to enter God's presence, but this way is not revealed as long as the outer tabernacle is still standing. What is this "outer tabernacle"? For the Jews, the outer tabernacle was the larger of the two rooms in the sacred tent. In this room we find the lampstand, the table, and the sacred bread (v. 2).

It was also the first room the priests entered as they ministered the daily worship service (v. 6). A second inner room was also in the tent. It is this inner room that the high priest entered just once a year (v. 7). This was the Holy of Holies, the dwelling place of God on the earth. In this room dwelt His manifest presence. God did not dwell in the "outer tabernacle"; He dwelt in the inner room.

The outer and inner rooms of the Jewish tabernacle symbolize our own outer and inner natures. Our "outer tabernacle" is our soul life, constituting the view of life as seen through the mind and emotions (the soul) of man. In the tabernacle of our soul, our focus is outward. Worship consists of something we "perform" through a proper adherence to the ritual of our particular form of service, according to our denomination or sect. It is that part of us that keeps us in church because of duty rather than vision. It leads us by our traditions instead of being led by the Spirit.

Rarely, if ever, does one experience the actual presence of the living God in the outer tabernacle. We may be saved by *faith*, but by *experience* the presence of God seems far removed. What is experienced is a myriad of different ideas, emotionalism (or lack thereof), and much confusion concerning church order, eschatology, and systems of worship. As long as man is ruled by circumstances rather than God, his "outer tabernacle" is still standing. No matter how zealous he seems, until the strength of his outer man is broken and an inner desire to worship and know God arises, the way into the holy place remains hidden.

Continuing the parallels between the Jewish tabernacle and human nature, the Bible tells us there was also an "inner tabernacle," which the Scriptures call the "Holy of Holies." This inner tabernacle corresponds to the spiritual side of man. As it was in the physical temple, so it is in the temple of flesh; the presence of God dwells in the inner tabernacle. In the physical temple, the inner tabernacle was so sacred, so holy, that great care was expended before it could be entered; no one casually entered the holy place. Into this Holy of Holies "the high priest enters once a year, not without taking blood, which he offers for himself and for the sins of the people committed in ignorance" (Heb. 9:7).

This inner tabernacle was the most sacred place on the earth, for the manifested presence of Yahweh, God of Israel, dwelt in this sacred room. When we think of entering the reality of God's presence, we are immediately confronted with the depth of our sinfulness. How shall we approach God and live?

Yet for us, the way into this holy place is not through self-improvement or any similar vain attempt. We enter the presence of God through our identification with Jesus Christ. God is not seeking to perfect *us*; He seeks to perfect our *relationship* with Jesus. He is our way into the Holy of Holies. He said, "No one comes to the Father but through Me" (John 14:6). Christ's expressed purpose is to bring us "to the Father." Most Christians place this promise in the hereafter. However, Jesus came to reconcile us to God in the *here and now* as well. Do not let this truth escape you!

The Scriptures tell us that "through Him we...have our access in one Spirit to the Father" (Eph. 2:18). The Word proclaims that we are "a holy temple in the Lord, in whom [we] also are being built together into a dwelling of God in the Spirit" (vv. 21–22). We are God's holy temple, His habitation in the Spirit, and it is "access...to the Father," where the Eternal One actually communes with us, that we are seeking.

Jesus said the Father is seeking worshipers. The worship that fully satisfies God must originate from the Holy of Holies, where the consciousness of man is awakened to the Spirit of God. Worship does not come from any system or form of service. Rather, it is the result of having truly discovered the Almighty One in "spirit and truth" (John 4:23).

# The New and Living Way

Because of sin and shame, every man places some sort of barrier between God and himself. The Bible refers to three instances of a veil separating the Jews from God. The first was the veil in the Hebrew temple. Here, only one man, the anointed high priest, and only once a year, could enter through the thick curtain (called the "veil") into God's holy place. This is the veil that was rent in two when Jesus died (Matt. 27:51). This barrier not only separated the outer room from the inner room of the tabernacle, *but it also separated the world of men from the presence of God.*

A second veil is mentioned: a veil Moses put over his face after having been with God. While Moses did have intimacy with God, the Jews begged the prophet to cover his face lest they see the glory of God, fading though it was (Exod. 34:29–35).

However, Paul tells of a third veil, less perceptible than the others and therefore more dangerous. This is the veil that remains unlifted, not only from the hearts of the Jews but also from all who know not God (2 Cor. 4:3–4). This is the veil of which the apostle says, "But whenever a person turns to the Lord, the veil is taken away" (2 Cor. 3:16).

This third veil is the veil of our self-life. When the veil of self cloaks our hearts, our perceptions are stained by the basic selfish orientation of our nature. But when one turns to the Lord, the veil of self-life, like the veil in the temple, is rent in two. This is not the cutting of cloth but the rending of the heart, the splitting in two of the tightly woven fabric of self-righteousness and self-consciousness. It is a violent rending, a putting to death, of the unregenerated self-nature.

Only if the old self-life is crucified without mercy or regret can the soul reach the state of purity where it begins to perceive, at last, the reality of God. In Moses we see a man *unveiled* before the presence of God. When Moses returned to the sacred tent, he would remove the veil from his face, turn, and step through the curtain of veils into the brilliant glory of God. Here, the Scriptures tell us, in the radiance of Eternal Life, Moses spoke to God face-to-face.

In like manner, *the very same sacred presence now dwells in the inner tabernacle of our spirits.* In Christ, with our veils of self, sin, and shame rent open, we too can turn and face God's glory—only the glory we face is not outside us. Nor does it fade from our faces as we depart from it. The Spirit of God dwells within us. And every time we truly behold Him, every time He is revealed to us, our hearts change in unending degrees of glory, transforming us into His same divine image from glory to glory (2 Cor. 3:18).

## The Veil of Christ's Flesh

In the light of such staggering spiritual realities, it is no wonder Satan fights the fulfillment of God's Word. The Father has provided a perfect offering, a sacrifice that for all time satisfies the penalty of sin. He has supplied an offering that enables us to enter "through the veil, that is [Christ's] flesh" into His glorious presence (Heb. 10:20).

You see, the final veil through which we pass is not made of linen; it is the fleshly body of Jesus Christ. We return to God through Him. The Scriptures tell us, "If we confess our sins, He is faithful and righteous to forgive us our sins and to cleanse us from all unrighteousness" (1 John 1:9).

The Word continues:

> My little children, I am writing these things to you that you may not sin. And if anyone sins, we have an Advocate with the Father, Jesus Christ the righteous; and He Himself is the propitiation for our sins.
>
> —1 JOHN 2:1–2

It is through Jesus's blood sacrifice that we are perfectly forgiven and thoroughly cleansed as we enter the presence of God. When Christ was resurrected, He entered into "the greater and more perfect tabernacle, not made with hands, that is to say, not of this creation" (Heb. 9:11). When Jesus entered this true heavenly tabernacle, of which Moses's tabernacle was a copy, He did not take the blood of goats and calves; *He took His own shed blood into the holy place* (vv. 12–14).

Again, the Book of Hebrews gives the best picture.

> Therefore even the first covenant was not inaugurated without blood. For when every commandment had been spoken by Moses to all the people…he took the blood of the calves and the goats, with water and scarlet wool and hyssop, and sprinkled both the book itself and all the people, saying, "This is the blood of the covenant which

God commanded you." And in the same way he sprinkled both the tabernacle and all the vessels of the ministry with the blood. And according to the Law...all things are cleansed with blood, and without shedding of blood there is no forgiveness.

—HEBREWS 9:18–22

Under the old covenant, Moses sprinkled the blood of sacrificed animals upon everything in the holy place. *Through the sprinkled blood he cleansed the basic uncleanness that exists in all created things.* What Moses did through the sprinkling of blood in the earthly tabernacle, Jesus has done for us with His own blood in the heavenly tabernacle.

Therefore it was necessary for the copies of the things in the heavens to be cleansed with [blood], but the heavenly things themselves with better sacrifices than these. For Christ did not enter a holy place made with hands, a mere copy of the true one, but into heaven itself.

—HEBREWS 9:23–24

Apart from you and me, there is nothing else in the heavenly tabernacle that is defiled. *We are the "heavenly things" that needed cleansing with Christ's blood before we could enter the true tabernacle.* As Moses cleansed the earthly copy of the holy place with blood, so Jesus cleanses the people who enter the true tabernacle with Him in Heaven.

During the Passover meal Jesus took the symbolic cup of wine and told His disciples, "Drink from it, all of you;

for this is My blood of the covenant, which is poured out for many for forgiveness of sins" (Matt. 26:27–28). Hebrews tells us this sacrifice was so perfect that "by one offering He has perfected for all time those who are [being] sanctified" (Heb. 10:14). When Jesus agreed to die for man, essentially what He said to the Father was, "Every time they sin and for every kind of sin they commit, as long as there is repentance and faith in their hearts, My life is given for their redemption."

> Therefore, brethren, since we have confidence to enter the holy place by the blood of Jesus, by a new and living way which He inaugurated for us through the veil, that is, His flesh, and since we have a great priest over the house of God, let us draw near with a sincere heart in full assurance of faith.
>
> —HEBREWS 10:19–22

The call and desire of God is for our worship to be in spirit and in truth. *Through the provision of Jesus Christ, we can be as close to God as our desires will take us.* The limits are not on God's side but on ours. With transcendent wonder and holy fear we can bow and worship in the reality of His Majesty. Through Jesus, we can draw near to God with a sincere heart in full assurance of faith; we can actually enter and abide in the holy place of God.

# PART SEVEN

## PURITY OF HEART

❧

It is possible in this world to walk purely before the Lord. In every generation a "little flock" receives the kingdom and goes on to fulfill the purposes of God for their generation (Luke 12:32). Everyone who is purifying himself, even as He is pure, is part of that little flock (1 John 3:3). They are pure because of love, not law. They are a bride making herself ready for her Husband (Rev. 19:7).

*Chapter 21*

# PURITY OF HEART: OPEN VISION

*Spiritual perception is based upon purity of heart. What we see in life and how we see it is rooted in the soil of our inner thought life. If we would experience clear and open vision concerning the kingdom of God, a pure heart is most essential.*

## Revelation Perception at the Throne of God

IN THE BOOK of Revelation there is a marvel: "...in the center and around the throne, four living creatures full of eyes in front and behind...around and within" (Rev. 4:6, 8). Our purpose here is not to spend ourselves in speculations about these creatures. Our goal is to possess that purity of heart that comes from living in the awareness of God. We're seeking the open vision that is manifested at His throne.

Though these "living creatures" may represent many things, one thing is certain: John was not seeing a nightmarish vision of six-winged beasts with dozens of eyes covering their bodies. What John saw was a symbol of a deeper truth. *The many "eyes" represent the open, all-inclusive vision that is the result of being in God's presence.*

Let it be known, where the Lord is, there also is His throne. If you've had a meeting with the Lord, it is because your spirit is at His throne. When you were spiritually reborn, you were born again *from above* (John 3:3, AMP). At this very moment, through the agency of the Holy Spirit, your spirit is "seated" with Christ upon His throne in heavenly places (Eph. 2:6). Where His presence is, there also is His throne; where His presence is, there also is open vision.

These "living creatures" are symbols of the life one finds as he abides in God's presence. In Him our eyes can *think*: they see with discernment and understanding. The mind of Christ fuses with our vision, revealing what was impossible to be seen by the narrowness of our perception; we see "in front and behind." Our vision also comes from "the center...[of] the throne." Not only do we see distant spiritual realities, but we are also close enough to penetrate and search the depths of God Himself (1 Cor. 2:10).

Yet, at the same time, being near to God also gives us "eyes...within," eyes that monitor the motives that guide self, inner eyes that stand guard against sin. The more our vision opens up, the greater we see God in His holiness. The slightest sin in our lives becomes significant; we are compelled to live pure before Him.

The "four creatures" at the throne of God do not cease to say, "Holy, holy, holy, is the Lord God, the Almighty" (Rev. 4:8). Day and night, God is holy. When our spiritual eyes are open, the utterances of our mouths are all, "Holy, holy, holy."

## A True Israelite Has Spiritual Perception

Jesus spoke concerning Nathanael, "Behold, an Israelite indeed, in whom there is no deceit!" (John 1:47). What kind of man was this young disciple, that *Jesus* should praise him? There was no guile, no deceit in this young man's heart. Oh, how we should desire this purity for ourselves! Nathanael had "eyes...within." He kept himself free from self-deception. *When you cleave to the truth inwardly, you will perceive the truth outwardly.* Nathanael looked at Jesus and declared, "You are the Son of God; You are the King of Israel" (v. 49).

Jesus said to Nathanael, "You will see greater things than these....I say to you, you will see the heavens opened and the angels of God ascending and descending on the Son of Man" (vv. 50–51). Because of Nathanael's honest heart, Jesus knew open vision was inevitable. Open vision is the consequence of a pure heart. To those who fight against sin, who hate falsehood, who diligently pursue walking in holiness, your struggle is a preparation for seeing God. You shall see the heavens opened.

Because of our dullness of heart, we have come to expect spiritual blindness as an unfortunate condition of this world. The truth is, in the Old Testament one of God's judgments against sin was that the heavens became "bronze." Most Christians similarly see the heavens closed. Few see with open vision either into the heavenly realms or into their own hearts. *The heavens are always "bronze" to a hardened heart.* But the Lord promised, "You shall see the heavens opened, and the angels of God"!

God wants us to have true spiritual vision. One sign that the Holy Spirit is involved in a church is that "young men...see visions, and your old men...dream dreams" (Acts 2:17). *There is continuity between God's kingdom in Heaven and His kingdom on the earth.*

Oh, there are those who say the supernatural was strictly limited to the first century, that today "we walk by faith, not by sight" (2 Cor. 5:7). Yes, we often do take steps of faith, where we walk without prior knowledge of what each step involves. *But we do perceive Him who is with us!* Ours is not a blind trust; it is a proven, seeing trust! Walking by faith and having spiritual vision is not an either/or situation. Just moments before Paul stated he walked by faith, he wrote, "We look...at the things which are not seen...things which are...eternal" (2 Cor. 4:18). Paul had *revelation perception of the spirit realm.* He saw the eternal spiritual body that was prepared and waiting for him in the heavens (2 Cor. 5:1, 4)! He knew how "a man...was caught up into Paradise and heard inexpressible words" (2 Cor. 12:3–4).

We could continue concerning Paul's spiritual perception, but the fact is, he authored one-third of the New Testament out of his open vision of Christ. How did he see the things he saw? Just after he declared "with unveiled face [we behold]...the glory of the Lord" (2 Cor. 3:18), he wrote, "But we have renounced the things hidden because of shame" (2 Cor. 4:2). Later he continued, "Having these promises, beloved, let us cleanse ourselves from all defilement of flesh and spirit, perfecting holiness in the fear of God" (2 Cor. 7:1). Out of a purified heart, out of his perfected holiness, came open vision of the glory of God.

Remember, we are not seeking experiences; we are seeking a pure heart. We are not running after visions; we want holiness. Even as the supernatural realm was an expected phenomenon in the primitive church, so also was purity the expected condition in their hearts. Therefore do not be as the foolish ones who seek visions. You must seek sanctification, and when you are ready, if God wills, He shall speak to you in supernatural ways (Acts 2:17–18). Do not seek to conjure up an "experience" with Jesus; seek to have a clean heart, allowing Christ to examine and purge you daily. And as He washes you with His Word and chastens you with His holiness, He will draw you into His presence. He will open your eyes to "things without and things within."

*Chapter 22*

# THE VIRGIN SHALL
# BE WITH CHILD

*The Bible is a book of reversals. Old things become new, the dead come to life, the lost are found. Even those who were the vilest of sinners are now empowered by grace to become the virgin bride of Jesus Christ.*

## The Virgin Bride of Christ

WE ARE CALLED to become a holy bride, the spotless wife of Jesus Christ. But before we become a bride, we must first become a virgin. In the Bible a virgin was not just one who was free from the sins of premarital sex or immoral behavior; a virgin was also "one set aside for another." The sense in which the church is to become virginal involves being uncorrupted, pure, and undefiled by the world. It implies being untouched by man's ideas, traditions, or sinfulness. To reach the goal of spiritual virginity, we must first be perfectly consecrated, wholly set apart for Jesus (2 Cor. 11:2–3).

Like everything in true Christianity, the purity of the church is not that which originates from herself; it is that which is imparted as virtue from Christ. It is true, living virtue, but it is Christ's virtue. Jesus, you will remember, was also a virgin. He had set Himself aside for us.

Indeed, it is with reference to Christ's union with the church, the marriage ceremony of the Son of God and man, that Paul wrote:

> For this reason a man shall leave his father and mother and shall be joined to his wife, and the two shall become one flesh. This mystery is great; but I am speaking with reference to Christ and the church.
>
> —EPHESIANS 5:31–32

Christ and His church: the *two* become *one* flesh! The apostle said, "This mystery is great." Do not presume you understand this just because you can read. This mystery is *great*. Jesus left His positional privileges as God's Son and clothed Himself in human flesh so that, through our spiritual rebirth, He might absorb mankind into His nature: the two became one! Jesus will always be the Son of God, but in love He chose to cleave unto His wife, the church. And while He is forever one Spirit with the Father, He is forever *married* to the church. Indeed, has this not been the eternal purpose of God: to bring the Spirit of His Son into the church, thereby creating man in both the divine image and the divine likeness (Gen. 1:26)?

Scripture calls Jesus Christ the last Adam (1 Cor. 15:45). He is the firstborn of the new creation as Adam was the firstborn of the old creation. The first Adam, however, in cleaving unto Eve, fell with her in sin. But Christ, in cleaving unto His church, has redeemed us and raised us up, seating us with Him in the heavenly places (Eph. 2:6).

The marriage of Adam and Eve, where Eve literally emerged and was born out of Adam's substance, is a prophetic type of the church born out of the actual substance of Christ. Paul tells us that our *bodies* are the physical members of Christ (1 Cor. 6:15; 12:12). We are not simply metaphorically the body of Christ, but spiritually we are "bone of [His] bones, and flesh of [His] flesh" (Gen. 2:23).

This truth is not New Age theology; it is not heresy. It is the unalterable Word of God. Christ Himself is *in* us. To believe otherwise is heresy. The test of Christian orthodoxy, according to Scripture, is in 2 Corinthians 13:5:

> Test yourselves to see if you are in the faith; examine yourselves! Or do you not recognize this about yourselves, that Jesus Christ is in you—unless indeed you fail the test?

We must recognize this about ourselves: Jesus Christ is in us. Yes, it is heresy to say we are Christ. Yet it is also error to deny He is within us. Paul expressed this mystery when he wrote:

> I have been crucified with Christ; and it is no longer I who live, but Christ lives in me; and the life which I now live in the flesh I live by faith in the Son of God, who loved me and gave Himself up for me.
>
> —GALATIANS 2:20

# The Preparation of Christ's Humanity

Christ Himself is in us. However, for Him to come forth *through* us, we must become a pure virgin. Revival comes as Christ prepares for Himself a people; as He is raised up within them, He draws all men unto Himself. Their Christlikeness is a door through which Jesus Himself enters the world.

"Therefore, when He comes into the world, He says, 'Sacrifice and offering You have not desired, but a body You have prepared for Me'" (Heb. 10:5). While descriptive of Christ's first coming, this verse is also applicable of His presence during revival.

Secure this thought in your mind: when the Spirit of Christ comes into the physical world, He must enter through a physical body. As was stated, the people or "body" Christ uses, of necessity, must be holy. They will have been prepared, set apart for Him beforehand. The purpose of that body is not to offer ritual sacrifices typical of the time and customs of the people. Rather, when Christ enters the world, through them, He repeats His eternal purpose: "I have come...to do Your will, O God" (Heb. 10:7).

We must not despise this time of preparation. Jesus Himself lived for thirty years before He was revealed and empowered as the Messiah. Although Jesus was always the Son of God, He "kept increasing in wisdom" (Luke 2:52). He could not learn of the kingdom of God in the rabbinical colleges of His day, neither could any man teach Him the mystery of the miraculous. All this had to come directly from the Father Himself. Jesus was

143

always sinless and obedient, but Hebrews 5:8–9 tells us, "Although He was a Son, He learned obedience from the things which He suffered...having been made perfect." The destiny the Father planned for Christ was something Jesus grew into, just as we must.

Hebrews plainly reveals Christ as the preexistent Creator; He is God from all eternity (Heb. 1:8). Yet, in the unfolding of Christ's earthy life, there was a point *in time* when His Messianic calling was announced from Heaven, where it commenced on the earth. Until He was baptized by John, Jesus had been in "labor" to bring forth His destiny, "pregnant" with the promise of God within Him.

After the water baptism, while Jesus was praying, the Spirit descended visibly upon Him in power, Heaven opened, and out thundered the voice of the Father: "You are My beloved Son..." (Luke 3:22). And all those promises and dreams, prophecies and visions, the thirty years of learning obedience and becoming acquainted with grief, stood poised in perfect surrender, focused upon this one incredible moment in time: "...in You I am well-pleased" (v. 22). Instantly the power of Heaven flowed into the spirit of Jesus, and the ministry of the Messiah was birthed.

The voice of God spoke, not to the crowds, not only for the sake of John the Baptist, but to Jesus. The requirements and days of preparation were fulfilled. In that eternal moment the Father said to Jesus, "Today I have begotten You" (Heb. 1:5; 5:5).

# Mary, a Type of the Church

In another sense, Mary, the mother of Jesus, also was "a body [God has] prepared" (Heb. 10:5). When Christ first entered our world as an infant, it was Mary whom God chose to give Christ birth. *Mary's life symbolized the qualities the church must possess to walk in the fullness of Christ.* She was humble, considering herself a bond-servant of the Lord; she unwaveringly believed the word spoken to her (Luke 1:34–38). And Mary was a virgin. These traits qualified her to be used by God in carrying, and giving birth to, Christ.

Like Mary, our humble state as the Lord's bondslaves is but a preparation for the coming forth of Christ in our lives. Yes, we have been "chastened" of the Lord. However, the goal of the Lord's chastening is not merely to punish; He seeks to make us *chaste*: pure and spiritually flawless. Indeed, our purity, our spiritual virginity as the body of Christ, is nothing less than God Himself preparing us, as He did Mary, to "give birth" to the ministry of His Son. Even now, in the spiritual womb of the virgin church, the holy purpose of Christ is growing, awaiting maturity, ready to be born in power in the timing of God.

# Embracing the Pains of Birth

We live within a time frame the Bible calls the "period of restoration" (Acts 3:21). Since the Reformation, the truth of Christ has been progressively restored to His church. Since the dark ages of apostasy, every time Christ's presence has been more fully revealed, it is because "a virgin church" has been in labor to bring Him forth. The Holy

Spirit impregnates a Martin Luther or a John Wesley—a person who God knows will continually say yes to Him—with a vision of the living God. The vision spreads to others, where it is tested with persecutions and refined with fire, but it spreads. Yes, those people are flawed. Truly, not a one of them is perfect. But along the way their vision of God possesses their souls. They become the "woman clothed with the sun," the virgin church who is "in labor and in pain to give birth" (Rev. 12:1–2).

As her hour nears, this virgin church lays aside her many tasks to focus on her one great commission. Through intense prayer and the agonizing of the Holy Spirit, in groanings too deep for words, she embraces her appointed destiny—until the very voice of Christ Himself is heard through her prayers: "Lo, I have come to do Your will, O God!" Birthed in His Spirit and in His power, fused together through love and suffering, this holy people become, as it were, a "body [God has] prepared."

Even now, hell trembles and the heavens watch in awe. For I say to you, once again the "virgin is with child."

> Before Jesus Himself returns, the last virgin church shall become pregnant with the promise of God. Out of her travail the body of Christ shall come forth, raised to the full stature of its Head, the Lord Jesus. Corporately manifested in holiness, power, and love, the bride of Christ shall arise clothed in white garments, bright and clean. During this last and greatest move of God, great darkness shall cover the earth. Even as in the judgment of Egypt, it will be a "darkness that can be

felt." Yet, in the midst of darkness, the visible, powerful glory of the Lord Jesus shall rise upon the virgin church. His glory shall be seen upon them. Nations shall be drawn to their light, kings to the brightness of their rising. Radiant shall they appear, for their hearts shall possess the beautiful star of the morning. In holy array, from the womb of the dawn, their light shall exult like the dew!

—ADAPTED FROM EPHESIANS 4:13;
REVELATION 2:26–27;
EXODUS 10:21;
ISAIAH 60:1–3;
2 PETER 1:19;
PSALM 110:1–3

# In Closing...

LET US NOT forget that the "kingdom of God does not consist in words but in power" (1 Cor. 4:20). Words, by themselves, are an illusion. They are merely the labels we use to define reality; they are not the reality they represent. Remember, the major difference between the kingdom of God and traditional religion is that the kingdom possesses in substance what religion has only in words.

Our goal is to seek and to find the holiness that leads us into the true presence of God. Let us also bear in mind that the Lord dwells in a secret place. No book, no teacher, no individual can discover for us what God's love demands we find for ourselves. If we know that we should seek God, we are debtors to our knowledge until we find Him.

Finally, simply do what you know to do. If you stumble, get up. If you sin, repent. Whatever you do, in spite of your feelings, do not lose your vision of Christlikeness. Your vision is your surest hope. Guard it. If you are faithful to your goal of Christlikeness, God will give you the grace to live in His presence. And when Christ, who is your life, is revealed, you also will be revealed with Him in glory (Col. 3:3–4).

—FRANCIS FRANGIPANE

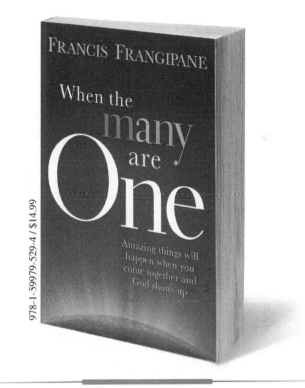

Made in the USA
Las Vegas, NV
17 December 2020

13759341R00090